An I   nd

F

ROWMAN & LITTLEFIELD EDUCATION
A division of
ROWMAN & LITTLEFIELD PUBLISHERS, INC.
Lanham • New York • Toronto • Plymouth, UK

Published by Rowman & Littlefield Education
A division of Rowman & Littlefield Publishers, Inc.
A wholly owned subsidiary of The Rowman & Littlefield Publishing Group, Inc.
4501 Forbes Boulevard, Suite 200, Lanham, Maryland 20706
www.rowman.com

10 Thornbury Road, Plymouth PL6 7PP, United Kingdom

British Library Cataloguing in Publication Information Available

Library of Congress Cataloging-in-Publication Data

Library of Congress Cataloging-in-Publication Data Available
ISBN 978-1-61048-649-1 (cloth : alk. paper) -- ISBN 978-1-61048-650-7 (pbk. : alk. paper) -- ISBN 978-1-61048-651-4 (electronic)

The paper used in this publication meets the minimum requirements of American National Standard for Information Sciences Permanence of Paper for Printed Library Materials, ANSI/NISO Z39.48-1992.

Printed in the United States of America

Table of Contents

Foreword

It is time to redefine the term *adjunct faculty*. In reviewing the definitions of *adjunct* the following descriptions are used: "something added," "not essential to it," "lesser status, rank," "without having full or permanent status." Do these descriptors accurately define *adjunct faculty* in today's world of higher education? I think not.

In 1960, 75 percent of college professors were full time; in 2010 only 27 percent of college faculty professors were full time. No longer do the terms *not essential* and *lesser status* apply. We are beginning to view adjunct faculty not as "something added" but rather as "value added."

An intent of Dr. Wong's book *An Instructor Primer for Adjunct and New Faculty: Foundations for Career Success* is to provide a practical guide to understanding the art and practice of teaching in higher education. The primary role of the professor is to teach. This may sound simple, but when placed within the context of higher education it is a complex and demanding responsibility that requires experience, knowledge, and a skill base that enhances the facilitation of learning.

This book identifies the various facets in becoming an effective faculty member. Dr. Wong provides not only direction and ideas of the teaching process itself but also an overview of the role and status of faculty in higher education.

An Instructor Primer for Adjunct and New Faculty: Foundations for Career Success is the most comprehensive treatment of the roles and responsibilities of the faculty—regardless of whether the person is new or adjunct—that I have read. What is particularly noteworthy is that the book is both insightful and practical. Dr. Wong has significantly reframed our understanding of what it means to be an effective faculty member in an institution of higher education.

University faculty members face many challenges. *An Instructor Primer for Adjunct and New Faculty: Foundations for Career Success* provides a practical guide to identifying, meeting, and exceeding these challenges.

Stephen Nunes, Ed.D.
Director, Center for Lifelong Learning
Moser College for Adult and Professional Studies
Benedictine University

Introduction

You have gone through many years in the classroom to get to where you are today. You have seen professors teaching in front of a class in various ways. There is one thing that you are sure about: it is professors and teaching. During your many years in the classroom you have viewed teaching through the lens of a student. The teaching story from the student point of view is only half-baked because it does not tell you everything you need to know about college teaching.

The story of the blind men and an elephant is a good metaphor to illustrate what students see about teaching. In various versions of the story, several blind men touch an elephant to learn what the animal is like. Each man feels only one part of the elephant, such as the side, the tail, the tusk, and the trunk. The blind men then compare what they "see," and they are in total disagreement. In a similar way the students are the blind men in the story. In this book, you will look at teaching from the professor's side of the classroom, a definitely different way of looking at college teaching.

The conventional wisdom that the academically able people make the best professors is often not accurate for the simple reason that the professors deal not only with content knowledge but also with people. The best and brightest professionals are coming more and more into higher education to do scholarly work—teach and research. They are highly capable, and sometimes even more so than their fellow classmates in the graduate and post-graduate programs. Some very academically able people who go into college teaching are used to achieving tasks that they do by themselves. But it is a completely different matter to help other people such as students to succeed. Teaching success does not depend solely on the isolated effort of a person. It depends critically on how well the professors can motivate students to work at learning on their own or with other people.

Some of you are reading this book because you are interested in learning more about what it is like to teach at the college level. Some of you reading the book may be considering a career decision with questions like "Is teaching right for me?" "Do I want to be a college teacher?" "What is my next career move?" I hope you will find answers to these questions in this book.

To some of you teaching may very well become a lifelong career that gives you joy and satisfaction because you get paid for your passion to read, write, teach, and research for the rest of your life. Bring your expertise and enthusiasm, and welcome to the teaching world of higher education.

Ovid K. Wong, Ph.D.

Chapter One

Welcome to the Teaching World of Higher Education

So you have an interest in teaching! Well, get ready to learn about the most rewarding vocation that will hopefully transform your current interest into a burning passion for sharing your knowledge and making a difference in the lives of your students.

—Frank T. Corso

ANTICIPATORY QUESTIONS

- What are the rankings and responsibilities of professorship?
- What are the challenges and rewards of teaching in higher education?

Cora is a staff-development executive of a city bank. She reads the following advertisement in a recent higher education online job posting with great interest:

Paine College invites applications from individuals interested in working as adjunct faculty in the English and literature areas. Paine College is located in Augusta, Georgia. The campus is located one hour away from Colombia, the capital of South Carolina. The mission of Paine College, a church-related private institution, is to provide a liberal arts education of the highest quality that emphasizes academic excellence, ethical and spiritual values, social responsibility, and personal development to prepare men and women for positions of leadership and service in the community, the nation, and the world.

Adjunct faculty members at Paine College are expected to teach undergraduate courses, which may include evening, weekend and/or on-line courses, and engage in teaching practices with an acute focus on documenting learning.

1

Individuals with terminal degrees in the disciplines offered at Paine College are invited to apply for these professionally engaging opportunities.

Additional qualifications include: innovative and successful integration of technology to impact student learning, skills in assessing student learning, and the ability to communicate effectively with a culturally diverse community. Successful candidates must be willing to participate in periodic professional development designed to maintain the academic quality of all programs.

Submit the following materials to be considered for inclusion in the pools of individuals certified to serve as adjunct faculty members at Paine College: Letter of application that details the applicant's expertise and outlines the applicant's qualifications for the position; curriculum vitae, a one page statement of teaching philosophy, three letters of recommendation, and official transcripts from institutions of higher education attended by the applicants." (HigherEdJobs.com, 2011)

Cora is not unique in her search for an adjunct faculty position to satisfy the desire to teach, and the Paine College job posting is not atypical of institutions of higher education recruiting to hire adjunct faculty. What prompts professionals like Cora to look for an adjunct faculty position? Predicated on the motivation, people interested in adjunct faculty positions may fall into one of the four following categories.

The majority of the first group of all adjunct faculty members is employed full time outside of academe and can best be categorized as professionals. Professionals find opportunities to fulfill themselves through sharing (i.e., teaching) their expertise. However, there are individuals in the second category who are fully retired or have reduced their full-time work hours so they may have more time for leisure. In 2012, 34 percent of the people in a survey said that they will be able to retire before age 65 (*USA Today*, 2012). A good portion of retired people are actually looking for a change-of-scenery job such as teaching college part time. There are individuals in the third category who hold several part-time jobs to meet their multiple needs of life. There are yet other individuals in the fourth category who are highly trained in their areas of expertise and aspire to become full-time college professors when given the right opportunity.

All in all, the person who is either full-time employed, retired, about to retire, freelance, or an aspiring academic looking for an adjunct position may have one common denominator—the passion to teach and work with students.

PROFESSOR TAXONOMY 101

One needs to first know the intricate taxonomy of higher education teaching in the United States before understanding who are adjunct faculty, new faculty, and other classifications. In the United States teaching in higher education commonly occupies a number of positions in academia, typically as full professor, associate professor, assistant professor, and other designations to include adjunct professor.

One major difference between the other professor classifications (i.e., adjunct professor) and the full, associate, and assistant professor ranks is the tenure process. Tenure generally constitutes a "lifetime" employment protection of faculty from scientific, political, or social controversies. A professor can be tenured, tenure-track, or non-tenure-track. However, adjunct faculty is typically non-tenure-track.

The title of professor is used loosely to denote instructors teaching at the postsecondary level of education. Technically, it is only a subset of all college faculties. These instructors commonly start their careers as assistant professors, with subsequent promotions to become associate professors and finally full professors.

The rank of assistant professor is commonly held for a period of five to seven years, after which the person must attain tenure and promotion to the rank of associate professor. When tenure is awarded, the person is theoretically under lifetime employment protection. Unfortunately, if the person fails to attain tenure, he has to leave and find other employment opportunities.

The rank of associate professor is considered a midlevel faculty position. The rank is awarded after a substantial documentation of scholarly accomplishments to include teaching, publication, and service. On the other hand, a person may be hired as an associate professor without tenure. If an associate professor rank is awarded to a non-tenured person, the position is typically tenure-track to mean that the person will work down the road to earn tenure.

The position of professor is the highest academic rank in the United States. This rank is earned after an outstanding track record of scholarly accomplishment. Each promotional step from assistant to full professor may come with increased administrative duties. This shift of duties is usually offset by a decrease of teaching and research responsibilities.

Outside the arena of assistant, associate, and full professor positions is a larger collection of other professor designations, including research professor, visiting professor, lecturer/instructor, and adjunct professor. A research professor has the classical responsibility of doing research. In many universities, they are not eligible for tenure and they usually fund their salary through research grants. Similar to the tenure-track-faculty ranks, research professors can be classified as an assistant or associate rank. Professors with limited-time teaching contracts are referred to as visiting or term professors. Lastly, an adjunct professor is a part-time professor hired to primarily teach courses on a contractual basis.

The College of Optical Sciences at the University of Arizona, Tucson, has a long and robust list of adjunct faculty. These adjunct faculty members have professional association with Raytheon, NP Photonics, National Optical

Astronomy Observatory, GE Healthcare, 4D Technology, Lasermax, The Aerospace Corporation, Dmetrix Instruments, U.S. Food and Drug Administration Center for Devices and Radiological Health, and the list continues to include even a Nobel laureate physicist! This adjunct faculty list represents a wide range of experience from some of the world's most respected businesses and underscores the previous discussion that adjunct faculty members bring with them a wealth of knowledge, expertise, and experience.

Did you know that Barack Obama was an adjunct faculty member at the University of Chicago for twelve years before his presidency? He split his time between the prestigious law school and the Illinois senate before the election. Obama's students might know him as the professor of constitutional law; nevertheless, his professional association with the university is adjunct with an official title of senior lecturer.

WHAT'S IN IT FOR THE ADJUNCT FACULTY?

The previous Paine College job advertisement paints a fairly accurate picture of what the adjunct faculty job entails—teaching. The implication of the advertisement is that the position requires mainly teaching and therefore does not require publishing and other administrative duties. If what is important to adjunct teaching is student learning (and it is), then what professors do in the classroom is a means to an end rather than an end in itself.

Many adjuncts may perceive teaching merely as imparting knowledge or skills. If an adjunct has that perception, then he is ready to be tossed blind into a real-world classroom. In most cases, what the adjunct may not have is the critical mass of sameness that gravitates to the professor who may teach the same course, and repeat doing that many semesters in a row. The challenge of teaching remains: what worked one semester might not work again the next semester!

Then what exactly is teaching? There is a need to consider two sets of variables before teaching can be fully explained. The first set is related to, but separate from, teaching. The institutional support, the size of the class, the maturity of the students, the specific content of the course, and the passion of the professor toward the students, the subject, and his profession belong to the first set. The second set is related to the actual strategies in the classroom. Connectivity to students, subject matter expertise, and differentiated styles of instruction in essence are the gems of the second set. Due to the complexity of the interacting teaching variables, more detailed treatment of the topic will be discussed in the next chapters of the book.

WHAT ARE THE CHALLENGES AND REWARDS?

Some of the challenges reported by adjuncts are the feeling of disconnectedness and lack of commitment to the institution. Other concerns are lack of communication with the program and university, lack of recognition for contribution, and lack of opportunities for professional development (Dolan, 2011). Maguire (2005) found most faculty complaints were in the areas of administrative and technological support. Frequently, universities still function as though faculties are all or mostly full-time instructors despite the reliance on adjuncts. Compensation advancement, scheduling of faculty meetings, and workshops often fail to take into account the significant proportion of adjunct faculty employed by many universities. The not-so-good news is not always the case. At some institutions adjuncts are viewed as the lifeline of the organization (Sixl-Daniels, Williams, and Wong, 2006) and they are well-integrated and valued.

Ron, who teaches a college course in music composition, will suffer a 50 percent pay cut if he quits his day job. Ron is the lead violinist of the local symphony and he teaches part time at the community college. Adjunct professors like Ron who typically teach part time may face a greater risk for layoffs than full-time faculty because the tenure process does not protect adjunct positions. Many adjunct positions typically have no employee benefits such as medical insurance or limited professional-development opportunities. For that reason, other supplemental employment is a necessity. Despite the challenges of working as an adjunct, Ron continues to teach because he loves teaching, and doing that is invaluable to his personal musical pursuits.

Wait. There are exceptions to the "no benefits" rule of adjunct faculty. The State University of New York (SUNY) system has benefits for adjuncts because the SUNY system is unionized. The SUNY's benefits include selected medical plans, New York University (NYU) retirement plan, child care, and elder care. The University of Alaska pays adjunct faculty the employer portion of Social Security and Medicare insurance premiums, contributions to tax-deferred annuities to supplement retirement contributions, and a tuition waiver for a maximum of three credits per semester. Lastly, many other college adjuncts are eligible for applying for staff-development funds.

Due to the lower earnings of adjunct professors, many colleges in the United States are in the practice of hiring more adjuncts on a contractual basis to save costs. The reason for staffing flexibility is that it works very well with changing student enrollment. Part-time hiring may well be the management trend of the future if the nation's economy remains unstimulated. For college systems struggling with tight budgets, hiring part-timers is obviously irresistible. Flexibility works in two ways: one for the college and the other one for the adjuncts. Mary, an adjunct, has turned down almost as many teaching offers as she has accepted. Mary continues to work as an adjunct professor because she enjoys the flexibility of the job, which allows her to move around with her husband, who is a corporate national staff developer.

David is an All-But-Dissertation (ABD) student at a state university and has little idea when he will be able to complete his Ph.D. in education. He teaches part time at a community college while working on his dissertation. Dividing one's time between finishing a thesis while working as an adjunct professor to make ends meet is common among aspiring academics. David loves adjunct teaching because there is no administrative or research demand on him, as there is with regular faculty. Is this not a trade-off for teaching as adjuncts? David may also add his adjunct experience to prepare him to be full-time faculty down the road. In the scenario, David's love of teaching does not equate success with full-time employment.

A university course schedule lists forty-eight undergraduate course offerings in mathematics for the semester. Twelve (25 percent) courses are taught by full-time faculty, and thirty-six (75 percent) courses are taught by adjunct faculty. Of the thirty-six courses, eleven (23 percent) courses are taught by adjuncts identified by names, and twenty-five (52 percent) courses are taught by adjuncts anonymously identified as "staff." What does the course schedule suggest? The university relies heavily on adjuncts to teach (i.e., 75 percent) all of the courses with great staffing flexibility.

The institutional demands of faculty employment are hinged on the golden business standard of supply and demand. The faculty supply depends largely on the output (or supply) of graduate programs across the country. In the late 1960s, faculty positions were in demand because enrollment in colleges soared. However, the supply of faculty members was uneven across the academic fields. In the mid 1970s, there was an enrollment demand shift in certain academic programs. The job prospects differ tremendously based on the field of study. Professional fields like business, the sciences, and technology are in general less competitive than the social sciences or the humanities. Colleges and universities responded readily by adjusting the distribution of faculty positions. By 1975 the supply of liberal arts faculty overwhelmed the demand; thus many new Ph.D.s had to seek nonacademic positions.

Adjunct faculty positions currently make up more than half of all faculty positions in the United States (Hoeller, 2007). The University of Phoenix is one of the largest higher education providers in North America. It employs more than 90 percent adjunct faculty. The University of Phoenix hires an overwhelming number of adjuncts partly because of its online education strategy, which will be discussed later in chapter 8.

In the 2012 special issue of the *Chronicle of Higher Education*, a reporter (Wilson, 2012) proposed a bold schema for the academic workforce to include primarily two categories of faculty members. The first category would be a small component of tenure-track professors—those who earn doctoral degrees, do research, train graduate students, and teach advanced courses. The second category would be a larger component of full-time instructors to teach undergraduates, help advise them, keep up with developments in the field by reading and attending conferences, but they would do no research. Instead of earning Ph.D.s, like those on the tenure track, instructors could stop with a master's degree, as many in the adjunct teaching pool already do. The proposal is likely to satisfy those who prefer to train for full-time teaching positions rather than for tenure-track positions or vice versa all within the tightening budget of the institution.

In 1960, 75 percent of college professors were full-time or tenure-track, according to the *New York Times*. Currently, only 27 percent fit that description (*Daily Iowan*, 2010). The adjunct hiring phenomenon seems to support that some colleges are more than willing to hire adjuncts when there is plenty of work to justify hiring full-time faculty. The rate of adjunct employment rose in 2009 and peaked in 2010 (figure 1.1). The overall trend in the last three years still staggers over 500 percent growth. The overarching consensus from figure 1.1 suggests that adjunct teaching is the trend of higher education hiring of the future, and the future is now.

How will the adjunct hiring boom impact the hiring institution? One obvious impact that has been described is getting more with the flexibility of the teaching assignment and the cost-saving related to such flexibility. However, what is critical is the adjunct impact on research and servicing the students. What seems to be the connection? Full-time faculty carry the task of service (i.e., student advising/mentoring, committee work) and scholarship (i.e., research and publication) above and beyond teaching. When the number of adjuncts hired shrinks the hiring of more full-time teaching faculty, research, committee work, and service to the students is likely to be compromised.

WHAT IS YOUR DECISION ABOUT JOINING THE ADJUNCT FACULTY?

If you are an adjunct professor, then you have already made up your mind about being one. However, if you are still thinking about it, then there is a need to reevaluate your priorities and your career goals. Are you a professional looking for an adjunct position because you have a passion to impart knowledge and skills that you know best? Are you retired and feel that you still have the energy level to work with students? Do you enjoy what you can create in the classroom to help students learn? Do you love working in the academic environment and may use adjunct teaching as an apprenticeship to more permanent college-type jobs? Finally, there may also be other combina-

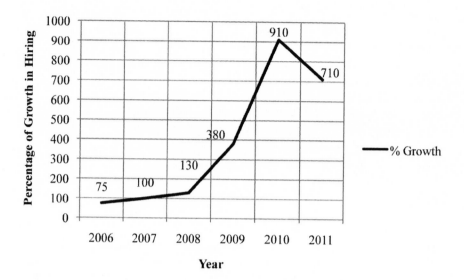

Figure 1.1. Adjunct Faculty Hiring Trends

tions of reasons for one to consider teaching as an adjunct faculty member. Regardless of the reasons, if you have the passion for college teaching, then being an adjunct faculty member could very well be the job of your life!

WHAT'S IN IT FOR THE NEW FACULTY?

If you are thinking seriously about or in the process of applying for a full-time college teaching position, you need to first and foremost understand the big picture of higher education employment. Are you not interested to know whether you are going into a job market on the rise or on the decline?

What follows is a summary of the 2012 U.S. Bureau of Labor Statistics (BLS) data on higher education employment and job-posting trends with HigherEdJobs.com.

1. The market share of higher education jobs compared to all other U.S. jobs continued to rise, notwithstanding at a slowing pace. Figure 1.2 compares the higher education jobs to all U.S. jobs from 2005 to 2012. Figure 1.2 is a chart with two y axes; one is a primary and the other is a secondary axis.

    The y primary axis on the right-hand side represents all U.S. jobs in the millions. 2007 is the peak year of all U.S. jobs, to be followed by the decline. The bottom of the curve is between 2009 and 2010. The graph is on the rise again after 2010.

The y secondary axis on the left-hand side represents higher education jobs. The number of jobs in higher education continued to grow at a slow-but-steady pace regardless of the trend in all jobs for the U.S. economy. Since 2006, higher education jobs share approximately 1 percent of all jobs in the country (Ikenberry, 2011).

2. The number of advertised job openings in higher education including employment at community colleges continued to grow in the 2009 postrecession economy. According to the BLS data, in 2011 there was an annual 11.5 percent increase in junior or community college job postings as compared to a 2.4 percent increase at four-year colleges and universities for the same period.

3. The number of full-time faculty postings went up since 2011and the postings continue to rise.

4. Colleges and universities continued to shift their faculty hiring from full- to part-time positions. All colleges and university faculty postings continued to shift slowly but surely toward part-time positions. The hiring trend reinforces the previous discussion in figure 1.1.

5. Higher education job postings went up in all geographical regions of the country. The increase is moderate in most areas. The mountain region was on top and the New England region was at the bottom of the job-posting chart. The Pacific, the Midwest, the Northeast, and the South are between the top and bottom extremes.

If you are a new faculty member, congratulations! What you are getting into will be exciting for five reasons. First, you have continuous human interaction in what you do. Second, you get respect for being an expert in your field.

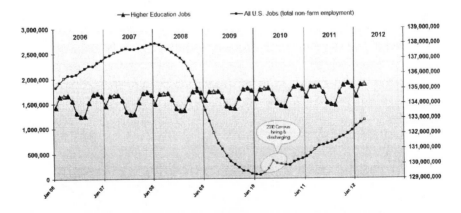

Figure 1.2.   Higher education jobs compared to all U.S. jobs (2006-2012) (source: HigherEdJobs based on U.S. Department of Labor Statistics data)

Third, you get intellectual stimulation and share the excitement. Fourth, you express creativity through teaching. Fifth, you make a difference in the advancement of knowledge and the lives of students.

This job is for you if you enjoy working with people, particularly with adult learners. A good part of the workday is in interacting with people. You never work in a silo, staring at a flat screen, or shuffling papers. You work with college students and they are fun and spontaneous. They will make your day when a student says, "I now understand the difficult concept that you helped me construct. The concept development is brilliant!" Or a student leaves an assorted box of chocolates in your mail slot and on it the card reads, "Thank you for the wonderful semester and Merry Christmas!"

This job is for you if you like your professional life to be enriched by the varied intellectual worlds of students. Students will make you feel that you are important as they embark on preparing themselves to be future productive citizens. When you do a good job, students will let you know. They will write a heartwarming note like "A professor teaches and a good professor makes learning enjoyable. Thank you for being a good professor."

This job is for you if you are excited by intellectual matters. If you wish to extend your college years in perpetuity, you are in for a treat. As a new faculty member you must have studied for years to transform from being a scholar to now a professor and this is only the beginning. Whether you decide to share your scholarly excitement "on top of a hill" or "on top of a mountain" depends on your ego.

Other ways to share the stimulation can be publishing research, publishing articles in professional publications, and attending and presenting at professional conferences. At a teaching university, more time is spent on teaching. On the other hand, at a research university the professor may teach less but still have a high expectation for research. In either a teaching or research university scholarly publication is the norm for tenure and promotion. Furthermore, how can you beat using your extended release times to continue your interest and further advance your academic stimulation and professional growth?

This job is for you if you are creative in expressing yourself. When you teach a lesson what you teach is the content or skills and how you teach is a way of expression. You can creatively build the lesson from multimedia programs to educational software, thus making the lesson delivery an exercise of creativity. Teaching is like playing a musical instrument, painting a picture, and singing a song. It is an art! If you enjoy teaching you know that you are exercising both your left (for logical thinking) and right (for creative thinking) brain. As always, many people conceive college professors to be liberals may be because they express their freedom in the academic profession in many creative ways.

This job is for you if you want to make a difference in someone's life. Teaching is much more than talking about knowledge. The best part of the teaching job is teaching students who care about learning. The professor can be exhausted before going to teach a three-hour class. The same person can come out all energized. Of course, the reverse is also true, that the worst part of teaching is teaching students who do not care about learning. Teaching is a noble profession that uses intellectual excellence to benefit others. Marcus Tullius Cicero (106–43 BC), a Roman statesman, said it well: "What nobler employment, or more valuable to the state, than that of the man who instructs the rising generation?"

WHAT IS THE REALITY?

In a recent national survey (Berrett, 2012) released by the Higher Education Research Institute at the University of California at Los Angeles, the majority of the faculty respondents felt stressed. The greatest source of faculty stress in descending order came from:

1. self-imposed high expectations,
2. lack of personal time,
3. working with unprepared students,
4. managing household responsibilities,
5. institutional budget cut,
6. institutional procedures and red tape, and
7. demands of research and publication.

Faculty members in the same national survey reported that they spent less time teaching (note: full-time faculty members teach on the average nine hours or more per week) and preparing to teach than in the past. Why? The decrease in the time spent teaching and preparing is evidence of the impact of higher education's growing reliance on adjunct faculty. As a matter of fact, full-time faculty have less time to devote to students because they have fewer people with whom to share the responsibility of shared governance, institutional service, and research.

Among the three areas on which full-time faculty performance is traditionally judged—teaching, scholarship (or research), and service—faculty members who took the national survey interestingly placed the highest priority on teaching. Unfortunately, faculty members also felt that they received little support in improving how they taught, which reinforces the thought that "teaching is much more than talking about knowledge."

One can assume that faculty remuneration is related to the value of the hiring institution. Did you know that the value of an institution rests heavily on its endowments? The total value of an institution is often referred to as the institution's endowment and is organized typically as a public charity, private foundation, or trust. The top five endowment universities in the country are Harvard, Yale, Princeton, the University of Texas System, and Stanford.

The field of needs is yet another factor that determines faculty remuneration. For example, certain professional fields such as health care and business are generally in more demand than fine arts or education.

Many institutions nowadays are student tuition and fees driven. For that reason, the tuition and fees structure may further suggest a frame of reference for faculty remuneration. Figure 1.3 is based on a selection of colleges and universities in Illinois. The University of Chicago is on top of the list and it is even more expensive than Harvard and Yale! Furthermore, the University of Chicago is among the top in the nation with reference to institutional endowment. What would be your remuneration expectation if you were to teach at the University of Chicago based on what you know about the institution?

	In state tuition & fees	Out-of-state tuition & fees
University of Chicago	$44,574	$44,574
Northwestern University	$43,779	$43,779
University of Illinois (Urbana-Champaign)	$14,522	$28,664
University of Illinois (Chicago)	$13,130	$25,520
Illinois Institute of Technology	$37,914	$37,914
DePaul University	$32,295	$32,295
Wheaton College	$30, 120	$30,120
Bradley University	$28,264	$28,264
Benedictine University	$25,850	$25,850
Northern Illinois University	$11,484	$20,377
Eastern Illinois University	$10,930	$27,670
Western Illinois University	$10,444	$14,450
Chicago State University	$ 9,966	$ 18,426
Illinois Central College	$ 3,195	$ 7,050
Illinois Valley Community College	$ 2,753	$ 7,986

Figure 1.3.   College tuition and fees in Illinois (2012-2013) (source: The Chronicle of Higher Education, November 2, 2012, Volume LIX, Number 10)

SUMMARY AND REFLECTION

Professionals seriously looking into teaching in higher education face challenges and rewards. One major reason for a professional to look into being a college teacher is the passion to teach and to work with students in an academic environment. The hiring trend of instructors for higher education (full or part time) has been on the rise for years and many colleges and universities are looking to hire more adjuncts to be flexible and cost effective.

Answer the following questions as a reflection.

1. How are the faculty members in higher education classified? What determines the classification?
2. What is the general job description of an adjunct professor?
3. What is the job perspective of adjunct faculty in the future?
4. What are the potential rewards for being a new faculty member? Are the rewards intrinsic or extrinsic? Please explain.

REFERENCES

Berrett, D. "Today's Faculty: Stressed, Focused on Teaching, and Undeterred by Long Odds." *Chronicle of Higher Education* 59, no. 10 (2012).

Daily Iowan Editorial Board. "Sharp Rise in Adjunct Professors Has Obvious Downsides." *Daily Iowan*, August 18, 2011. Accessed January 22, 2013. www.dailyiowan.com/2010/03/29/Opinions/16359.html.

Dolan, Vera. "The Isolation of Online Adjunct Faculty and Its Impact on Their Performance." *International Review of Research in Open and Distance Learning* 12, no. 2 (2011): 62–77.

HigherEdJobs.com. Job posting. Posted on November 1, 2010. Reposted on May 25, 2011. www.higheredjobs.com/details.cfm?JobCode=175525841

Hoeller, K. "The Future of the Contingent Faculty Movement." InsideHigherEd.com, November 13, 2007. Accessed January 22, 2013. http://insidehighered.com/views/2007/11/13/hoeller.

Ikenberry, J. "Higher Education Employment Report, Second Quarter, 2011." HigherEdJobs.com, August 2011. Accessed January 22, 2013. www.higheredjobs.com/documents/HEJ_Employment_Report_2011_Q2.pdf.

Maguire, P. (1984). *Continuous Quality Improvement in the Employment of Adjunct Faculty*: A NIACC Plan (Report No. JC960 1400). Mason City, Iowa: North Iowa Area Community College.

Sixl-Daniell, K., J. Williams, and A. Wong. "A Quality Assurance Framework for Recruiting Training (and Retraining) Virtual Adjunct Faculty." *Online Journal of Distance Learning Administration* 9, no. 1 (spring 2006). Accessed January 22, 2013. www.westga.edu/~distance/ojdla/spring91/daniell91.htm.

USA Today, September 7, 2012 (Source: Princeton Survey Research Associate International Survey of 1508 financial decision makers)

Wilson R. (2012) *The Chronicle of Higher Education*, October 19, 2012, Volume LIX, Number 8.

Chapter Two

Set the Stage before the First Day of Class

There is a direct correlation between teacher planning and what students learn. Planning is pervasive to the teaching process. For maximum results, planning is quintessential. In other words, planning is the purest avenue of generating the greatest student engagement and performance. Doing so makes the teacher's effort in the classroom count.

—Steve Fry

ANTICIPATORY QUESTIONS

- How do you prepare the work environment before starting the school term?
- How do you prepare yourself before starting the school term?

Do you remember your first blind date? Do you recall the anxiety and the anticipation? What came to mind? *How do I greet and impress the date? What if I say the wrong thing? What if I do not have enough money to pay since I do not yet have a credit card?* Blind dating is always exciting yet it is still a bit scary. Honestly, the first day of teaching college is not that much different.

You have been a college student yourself for many years and you know very well what college teaching is about. You have seen college professors stand and deliver in a large lecture auditorium. You also may have seen college professors teach with half of the class falling asleep. Imagine it is you now standing in front of a college classroom. If that thought alone does not pump your adrenaline, who knows what will.

Many aspiring college students strongly believe in the power of knowledge. Following that line of logic is the power of knowledge that transitions some from students to scholars and launches some of them eventually to a career in teaching at the college level. It is not difficult to understand that if the person has a vast knowledge of a subject, that person is prepared to teach college. The assumption is all well and good until we see academically well-qualified college professors doing less than a good job in teaching to support the perception that speaking knowledgeably does not necessarily represent good teaching.

There are a number of items that the adjunct faculty member needs to check before the first day of class. These items, not in any particular order, are the syllabus, the student roster, the classroom, the office (to include the portable office), and last but not least an understanding of his/her teaching philosophy to include learning style. An understanding and organization of the items mentioned will eventually come together to form the total work environment (i.e., both external and internal) of the faculty.

THE SYLLABUS

A course syllabus is generally handed to the faculty upon the signing of the work contract. The course syllabus is established by the college or the department and it is used as a legal document of teaching and learning. For that reason, the person given the teaching contract does not have the option of making major changes in the syllabus. In a nutshell, the syllabus is a description of the course to cover, contact information, course objectives, teaching schedule, deliverables, and accountability and deliverables guideline.

Are the required and supplemental (or recommended) books stated clearly in the syllabus? Is the course using the latest edition of the publication? It is a great idea to visit the college book store and see who is in charge if there are book questions. Be cognizant about the proper use of the books as you plan your teaching. College textbooks are very expensive. If you plan not to reference them in your teaching, you will hear from the consumers and students will say, "Why buy the textbook?" If you plan to teach directly from the books you will also hear from the consumers as students will say, "I can read!"

Study the course objectives of the syllabus carefully. Understand the teaching ramifications of the course objectives and ask yourself questions such as "Will I able to teach to the course objectives by the end of the school term?" and "How do I support the course objectives with purposeful knowledge and meaningful skills?" The answers to such questions may not be critical if the course contributes only to the general requirement of a degree program. However, it will be absolutely critical if it is a part of the preparation program for any professional certification program. In other words, not teaching to the course objectives is not preparing the student to take and pass the external examination required by the professional certification program.

Study the course teaching schedule of the syllabus carefully. Are you teaching a semester (sixteen weeks), a quarter (ten weeks), or a module/session (eight weeks)? How is the teaching of the course objectives spread over the allotted time in weeks? In education, scheduled teaching in a certain time allocation is called pacing. Is pacing reasonable, or is it too aggressive? If you are teaching the course for the first time, you may add a safety net by labeling it a tentative teaching schedule.

Students appreciate knowing what is ahead so they may prepare accordingly. Is a schedule of assignments and the due dates a part of the syllabus? Pacing of the assignment is as critical as the pacing of the teaching. Assignments might come in waves to reinforce the lessons. Are the assignment waves evenly paced? See to it that they are adjusted if the assignment schedule is tight at times.

Study the grading policy of the syllabus very carefully. Not understanding the policy might invite unnecessary challenges from students about work assessment and course evaluation. It is common to see grade distribution (sometimes in percentages) stated with reference to attendance and participation, class assignments, projects, the midterm, and the final examination. Are the cut scores for A, B, C, D, or F stated clearly in black and white? The grading policy of a course is developed commonly by the college or the department to achieve fair and consistent student evaluation. Try not to deviate from the set policy or be prepared to hear from your students and the administration.

Do not overlook other policies in the syllabus as they tell you exactly what to do in certain situations. Do you know what to do when a student is turning in late work, is chronically not coming to class, is caught cheating, asks you for extra time for taking a test, or is taking off due to religious obligations?

The syllabus is an agreement concerning matters of learning and teaching. This is the backdrop to ensure smooth operation between the students and the instructor. Students are satisfied when they know what is ahead for learning and the information should be in the syllabus. Use the syllabus to keep the students and the professor informed and avoid surprises.

Going back to the metaphor of the first blind date, the syllabus just might be the soda that you (the instructor) and your date (the student) sip from two drinking straws. The drinking straws are the two avenues that are used to draw from the same soda—the syllabus. Figure 2.1 is a sample syllabus. Can you identify the syllabus components described? What adjustments would you make to better suit your teaching purposes?

BENEDICTINE UNIVERSITY
EDUC 630
Educational Research Methods
Semester: Fall 20xx

Benedictine University's Conceptual Framework:

Benedictine University educators are effective practitioners, committed to scholarship, lifelong inquiry, leadership and social responsibility.

As a result of this course, you will be expected to demonstrate:
- scholarship by developing a firm understanding of the content of the course;
- lifelong inquiry by actively seeking out answers to your emerging questions;
- leadership by assuming roles that improve practice, such as initiating discussions, serving as a group leader, and volunteering;
- social responsibility by exploring ways to maximize the potential of all learners.

Instructors: Ovid K. Wong, Ph.D., Associate Professor
College of Education and Health Services, College of Science
ovidwong@benedictineuniversity.edu 834-123-4567

Office Hours: By appointment

Class Sessions: Kindlon Hall – Room #124
Monday – 6:30pm – 9:20pm

Required Texts: Mertier, C. A. & Charles, C. M. (2011). *Introduction to Educational Research* (7th Ed).
New Jersey: Pearson.

ISBN-10: 0131381148
ISBN-13: 9780131381148

Websites: **Illinois State Board of Education – www.isbe.net**
Council for Exceptional Children – www.cec.sped.org
U.S. Department of Education-www.ed.gov/-Federal

Recommended: *Concise Rules of APA Style.* (6th ed.). Washington, D.C.: American Psychological Association.

Course Description: This course focuses on research fundamentals and provides the student with an understanding of how to develop a proposal and conduct research in the educational field. In the development and execution of a research design, each student will (1) identify a problem to be investigated, (2) review the relevant literature, (3) formulate an appropriate methodology for the planned study (i.e., experimental, correlational, or qualitative), and (4) write up the thesis proposal in the appropriate APA publication style. To assist the student in these tasks, the instructor will discuss relevant sections from the required texts.

Course Objectives:

Upon completion of the course, the student should achieve the following:

1. be able to apply the basic principles of research design (which includes the statement of the research problem, formulation of the hypotheses, and notation of research importance) to quantitative or qualitative undertakings;

2. competently perform a literature review outline on a topic of research interest and merit to the educational field;

3. be able to apply a methodology to a given set of data which is appropriate to the demands of that method;

4. become comfortable enough with descriptive and inferential statistical techniques so that the data obtained from the thesis can be analyzed in a suitable fashion;

5. begin to explore the use of statistical computer programs in order to analyze and interpret data;

6. learn the standardized procedures for writing the components of the thesis according to the APA's (American Psychological Association's) publication style; and

7. develop competent presentation skills to present the thesis proposal to respective peers in the classroom.

Course Guidelines and Requirements:

Class Attendance and Late Work
- Class attendance from beginning to end of class and full, positive participation is expected. Repeated absences or any other practices that indicate lack of commitment to quality work or classroom interaction will impact your grade. Please notify the professors of emergency absences or tardiness via e-mail or voice-mail, prior to class.

Style Requirements
- All assignments are reviewed for grammar, mechanics, usage and spelling in addition to content. All written work completed outside of class is to be word processed, spell-checked, and edited prior to submission. Please adhere to the APA format for stylistic and reference guidelines. Back-up copies of computer files are expected and assignments submitted late due to computer or printer problems remain late assignments.

Grade Determination

The grading breakdown is as follows:
Thesis Proposal = 70%
Oral Reports = 20%
Attendance & Participation = 10%

The grading scale for each exam will be as follows:
90-100   A
80-89   B
70-79   C
60-69   D
Below 60 F

Tentative Schedule:

8/27	**Course Introductions** *Chapter 1: Educational Research: Its Nature and Rules of Operation*
9/3	*NO CLASS – LABOR DAY*
9/10	**Types of Research** *Chapter 2: Types of Educational Research and Corresponding Sources of Data*
9/17	**Types of Research** *Chapter 15: Action Research* *Chapter 16: Evaluation Research*
9/24	**Selecting a Research Topic** *Chapter 3: Selecting, Refining, and Proposing a Topic for Research*
10/1	**Literature Review** *Chapter 4: Locating Published Research*
10/8	*RESEARCH WEEK – Class will not meet; instructors will be available for individual appointments*
10/15	****Research Summary Presentations**** *Chapter 5: Interpreting and Summarizing Published Research*
10/22	**Problem Statements** *Chapter 8: Designing a Research Project*
10/29	*Individual Student Meetings: Problem Statement, Research Design Plan, & Updated Research Spreadsheet* ***Class will not meet***
11/5	**Specific Types of Research** *Chapter 10: Qualitative Research Methods* *Chapter 11: Survey Research* *Chapter 12: Nonexperimental Quantitative Research*
11/12	**Specific Types of Research** *Chapter 13: Experimental, Quasi-Experimental, and Single-Subject Designs* *Chapter 14: Mixed-Methods Research Designs*
11/19	**Gathering & Analyzing Data** *Chapter 6: Procedures and Tools for Gathering Data* *Chapter 7: Analyzing Research data and Presenting Findings*
11/26	**Analyzing Data & Preparing a Research Report** *Chapter 7: Analyzing Research Data and Presenting Findings* *Chapter 9: Preparing a Research Report*
12/3	*WRITING WEEK – Class will not meet; instructors will be available for individual appointments*
12/10	****Research Proposal Presentations & Report Due****

University Policy Statements

Academic Honesty:
Evidence of plagiarism; taking credit for work completed by another person or student in this class; or any other form of academic dishonesty will result in an F on the assignment in question or an F in the course depending upon the extent of the dishonesty.

Academic Honesty Policy
The search for truth and the dissemination of knowledge are the central missions of a university. Benedictine University pursues these missions in an environment guided by our Roman Catholic tradition and our Benedictine heritage. Integrity and honesty are therefore expected of all members of the University community, including students, faculty members, administration, and staff. Actions such as cheating, plagiarism, collusion, fabrication, forgery, falsification, destruction, multiple submissions, solicitation, and misrepresentation, are violations of these expectations and constitute unacceptable behavior in the University community. The penalties for such actions can range from a private verbal warning, all the way to expulsion from the University. The University's Academic Honesty Policy is available at **http:/www.ben.edu/AHP and students are expected to read it.**

Academic Support Services:
If you have a documented learning, psychological, or physical disability, you may be eligible for reasonable academic accommodations or services. To request accommodations or services, contact the Student Success Center in the KRASA Center, lower level, Room 012. All students are expected to fulfill essential course requirements. The University will not waive any essential skill or requirement of a course or degree program.

Religious Accommodations:

A student whose religious obligation conflicts with a course requirement may request an academic accommodation from the instructor. Students must make such requests in writing by the end of the first week of the class. Upon receiving such a request, the instructor will offer reasonable academic accommodations, whenever feasible, and communicate this to the student. However, the course requirements listed in the syllabus remain in effect if accommodations cannot be offered.

- [ ] **Chapter One**
  - o Statement of the Problem
  - o Importance of the Study
  - o Operational Definition of Terms

- [ ] **Chapter Two**
  - o Outline of Literature Review

- [ ] **Chapter Three**
  - o Hypothesis or Questions
  - o Participants
  - o Instrumentation
  - o Procedure Limitations
  - o Design
  - o Data Analysis

- [ ] **Chapter Four**
  - o Discussion of Anticipated Data

- [ ] **Chapter Five**
  - o Anticipated Summary
  - o Anticipated Conclusions
  - o Anticipated Recommendations

- [ ] **References (at least 30)**

- [ ] **Appendix**
  - o Consent Forms
  - o Information Forms

- [ ] **IRB Checklist**
  - o NIH Certification
  - o University Form
  - o All Attachments

- [ ] **Power Point on Thesis Proposal**

Master's Proposal -- Thesis Deadlines

Chapter 1: Introduction *(completed by end of 630 course)*
    Should include: Overview of Research Area,
            Statement of Problem
            Importance of Study,
            Operational Definitions of Terms,
            & Delimitations

Chapter 2: Review of Related Literature *(Outline only -- completed by end of 630 course)*

Chapter 3: Methodology *(completed by end of 630 course)*
    Should include:
            Hypotheses,
            Participants,
            Apparatus,
            Procedure
            Limitations of Study,
            Data Analysis

IRB - *(completed by end of 630 course)*

Chapter 4: Discussion of Data *(completed in next two semesters)*

Chapter 5: Summary, Conclusions, And Recommendations *(completed in next two semesters, along with selected references section, appendix, and abstract)*

**Defense of Action Research Proposal – *Based upon completion of thesis*

CONCEPTUAL FRAMEWORK
School of Education
Benedictine University

Benedictine University educators are
effective practitioners, committed to
scholarship, lifelong inquiry,
leadership and **social responsibility.**

These four strands are woven into the education curriculum and are reflected in the expectations we have for our graduates:

Scholarship
Benedictine University's education program requires that students have a firm understanding of the subject matter and a well-rounded background in sound pedagogical principles that promote understanding of the content. They stay abreast of research and technological advances and apply innovative strategies that enhance teaching and learning.

Lifelong Inquiry
Students readily approach issues and challenges in a proactive way by questioning and critically reflecting upon their current understandings. They seek out information, both individually and collectively, and formulate an in-depth knowledge base, grounded in research that informs their thinking and decision making.

Leadership
Benedictine educators are prepared for and willing to assume leadership roles that enable them to affect change and improve educational practice through the application of sound theory and ethical principles. They have learned how to be flexible, supportive, ethical and responsible and they use their knowledge to promote effective educational initiatives that enrich learning experiences.

Social Responsibility
Educators in Benedictine's programs are dedicated to creating fair and equitable environments that support and enhance the learning of all students. They are able to accommodate their teaching practices in order to address individual differences. They strive to maximize each person's potential by fostering self-esteem and motivation, and developing strategies that help learners deal with potential intellectual and social challenges. They promote professional relationships with others (colleagues, parents, agencies) to improve educational practice.

Illinois Professional Teaching Standards

#1 Content Knowledge
The teacher understands the central concepts, methods of inquiry, and structures of the discipline(s) and creates learning experiences that make the content meaningful to all students.

#2 Human Development and Learning
The teacher understands how individuals grow, develop, and learn and provides learning opportunities that support the intellectual, social, and personal development of all students.

#3 Diversity
The teacher understands how students differ in their approaches to learning and creates instructional opportunities that are adapted to diverse learners.

#4 Planning for Instruction
The teacher understands instructional planning and designs instruction based upon knowledge of the discipline, students, the community, and curriculum goals.

#5 Learning Environment
The teacher uses an understanding of individual and group motivation and behavior to create a learning environment that encourages positive social interaction, active engagement in learning, and self- motivation.

#6 Instructional Delivery
The teacher understands and uses a variety of instructional strategies to encourage students' development of critical thinking, problem solving, and performance skills.

#7 Communication
The teacher uses knowledge of effective written, verbal, nonverbal, and visual communication techniques to foster active inquiry, collaboration, and supportive interaction in the classroom.

#8 Assessment
The teacher understands various formal and informal assessment strategies and uses them to support the continuous development of all students.

#9 Collaborative Relationships
The teacher understands the role of the community in education and develops and maintains collaborative relationships with colleagues, parents/guardians, and the community to support student learning and well-being.

#10 Reflection and Professional Growth
The teacher is a reflective practitioner who continually evaluates how choices and actions affect students, parents, and other professionals in the learning community and actively seeks opportunities to grow professionally.

#11 Professional Conduct

The teacher understands education as a profession, maintains standards of professional conduct, and provides leadership to improve student learning and well-being.

Figure 2.1 A Sample Syllabus

THE STUDENTS

Study the student roster carefully. The roster tells the class size, the student names, and the student contact information such as address, telephone number, and email. More importantly, the roster identifies the student levels in terms of freshmen, sophomores, juniors, and seniors. Typically, freshmen have undeclared majors; unfortunately, this is another way of saying that the student doesn't know what to pursue in college. To many college teachers, teaching a class of freshmen is not much different from teaching a group of high school students! Juniors and seniors mostly have declared majors, and these students are typically more focused in their pursuit of career and academic goals. From the student roster one may prepare the grade book to include attendance, coursework, and name cards possibly for a seating chart.

THE CLASSROOM AND OFFICE

A visit to the classroom before the first day of class is always helpful. Are the desks and chairs movable, or are they fixed to the floor? Flexible classroom furniture arrangement is conducive to various ways of lesson delivery. On the other hand, if the furniture cannot be rearranged, then the instructor will be less flexible in his/her ways of lesson delivery. Are you a tech person? Do you use equipment to assist you in teaching? Do you know how to use the various pieces of equipment if they are already in the room? Do you know what username and password to use to access the college share drive to get to your teaching resources? Or do you have to bring your own equipment every time you come in to teach?

Do not forget to stop by the office before the first day of class. You may have a work space or an office. Do you know the person in charge of the office to request support services such as copying and purchasing? Where is the office mailbox and places that you get supplies such as pencils, notepads, paper clips, staples, paper, markers, adhesive tape, correction fluid, rulers, and so forth?

If you are an adjunct, do not despair if you do not have your own office because you can still get things done in a portable office—office-in-a-box. After all, isn't "portability" a part of the adjunct job description? A typical office-in-the-box is a plastic box with a carrying handle. The box has hanging files for the syllabus, handouts, returned assignments, class rosters, pens, erasable markers, and erasers, and so on. Make sure that the file folders are labeled for organization and easy access. The office-in-a-box works the following ways:

1. Check the syllabus on a regular basis to make sure that the teaching is on target.
2. Does the class roster reflect the attendance and the work of the students? Write notes to the students if there are issues in this area. Do not dawdle.
3. Check the handouts and align them with the lessons.
4. Make sure that the assignments folder is current. Missing assignments should be marked accordingly and graded assignments should be returned quickly after grading.
5. The teaching supplies such as the markers and pens are fresh and usable.

THE PROFESSOR

In addition to being a knowledge expert, the professor needs to know himself well before the first day of class, especially if this is his first time teaching.

The philosophy of knowing oneself goes back some 2,500 years when Sun Tzu, a well-recognized Chinese military strategist, said, "Know yourself and know your enemy. You will be safe in every battle. You may know yourself but not the enemy. You will then lose one battle for every one you win. You may not know yourself or the enemy. You will then lose every battle" (Gagliardi, 2003). In the classroom, the essence of knowing oneself is to know one's disposition in teaching. Study and complete the two surveys below to find the two important traits of an effective professor: educational philosophy and learning style.

Study the following educational philosophy survey (table 2.1) to determine what you truly believe in teaching—your philosophy. For each statement there is a selection of *strongly disagree* (worth 1 point), *disagree* (worth 2 points), *neutral* (worth 3 points), *agree* (worth 4 points), and *strongly agree* (worth 5 points). What you score in items 2, 7, 8, and 11 indicates your total score of an adult-run educational philosophy. Your total score in items 4, 9, 10, and 12 indicates your total score of a student-run educational philosophy. Finally, your total score in items 1, 3, 5, and 6 indicates your total score of a collaborative educational philosophy. Your score for each educational philosophy may vary. A high score shows a strong preference for that philosophy. What is your predominant educational philosophy based on your score of the survey? Do you see a little bit of yourself in each educational philosophy?

Respond to the twenty-four statements about learning in table 2.2. For each statement there is a selection of *often* (worth 6 points), *sometimes* (worth 4 points), and *seldom* (worth 2 points). In table 2.3, add up the points in each column to calculate the total score under each heading when you are

1. A student who may not read on his own but loves to be read to asks adults to read books to him, and discusses readings with other people, is a more advanced learner in reading than a student who reads fluently by himself but hates and avoids reading.
   strongly disagree   *(1)*   *(2)*   *(3)*   *(4)*   *(5)*   *strongly agree*

2. The purpose of classroom management is to make sure that the students do exactly what the teacher want and expects them to do.
   strongly disagree   *(1)*   *(2)*   *(3)*   *(4)*   *(5)*   *strongly agree*

3. The teacher should give students a choice of classroom activities and negotiate what the students want to do and what the teacher has in mind for them to do.
   strongly disagree   *(1)*   *(2)*   *(3)*   *(4)*   *(5)*   *strongly agree*

4. The teacher should avoid providing answers to the students in order to not inhibit the students' thinking, learning, and creativity.
   strongly disagree   *(1)*   *(2)*   *(3)*   *(4)*   *(5)*   *strongly agree*

5. The teacher and students should set classroom rules and expectations together as a way of sharing problem-solving among all class participants.
   strongly disagree   *(1)*   *(2)*   *(3)*   *(4)*   *(5)*   *strongly agree*

6. Teaching involves sharing interests between the teacher and the students and among students with the teacher guiding this process of sharing.
   strongly disagree   *(1)*   *(2)*   *(3)*   *(4)*   *(5)*   *strongly agree*

7. If students aren't given incentives, they will not be motivated to learn in school.
   strongly disagree   *(1)*   *(2)*   *(3)*   *(4)*   *(5)*   *strongly agree*

8. Teaching is about transmitting knowledge and skills from the teacher to the students.
   strongly disagree   *(1)*   *(2)*   *(3)*   *(4)*   *(5)*   *strongly agree*

9. The teacher should never use extrinsic motivation to promote student learning.
   strongly disagree   *(1)*   *(2)*   *(3)*   *(4)*   *(5)*   *strongly agree*

10. The students mainly learn by osmosis and by their discoveries in the classroom learning activities.
    strongly disagree   *(1)*   *(2)*   *(3)*   *(4)*   *(5)*   *strongly agree*

11. The teacher has to make sure that first the students learn rules and skills for the target practice and only then their applications.
    strongly disagree   *(1)*   *(2)*   *(3)*   *(4)*   *(5)*   *strongly agree*

12. Interesting learning activities in the classroom will take care of classroom management without much teacher intervention.
    strongly disagree   *(1)*   *(2)*   *(3)*   *(4)*   *(5)*   *strongly agree*

Table 2.1. Educational Philosophy Survey

finished with all the responses. Are you predominantly a visual learner, an auditory learner, or a tactile learner? Will your learning profile affect the way you teach? The answer is affirmative. Typically, you tend to teach the way you prefer to learn and this is another important part of knowing yourself.

Finally, regardless of your personal philosophy of teaching (i.e., adult centered, student centered, or collaborative) and your learning style (i.e., visual, auditory, tactile), you need to nourish the following culture in the classroom:

1. Be emotionally present for your students. It is a powerful message of respect that improves communication and reinforces relationships.

Visual		Auditory		Tactile	
Number	**Points**	**Number**	**Points**	**Number**	**Points**
02	_____	01	_____	04	_____
03	_____	05	_____	06	_____
07	_____	08	_____	09	_____
10	_____	11	_____	12	_____
14	_____	13	_____	15	_____
16	_____	18	_____	17	_____
19	_____	21	_____	20	_____
22	_____	24	_____	23	_____
Total	_____	**Total**	_____	**Total**	_____

Table 2.2. Learning Style Inventory

2. Have fun doing what you are doing. Tap into your natural way of being creative and having fun. Having fun is the spirit that drives the curious learning mind, as in "Let's play with that idea!" This should be a mindset that the professor brings to everything he does.
3. Find ways to serve or delight students in a meaningful way. Make their day! It is all about contributing to someone's life, not because you want something out of it, but because that is the person you want to be.
4. Take responsibility for how you respond to what life throws at you—good, bad, or indifferent. Choose your attitude. Once you are aware that your choice impacts students in the classroom, you can ask yourself, "Is my attitude helping my students?" or "Is my attitude helping me to be the person I want to be?" Only through this work philosophy can the professor build stronger relationships with the people he works with, and the students he teaches.

Do you feel that, historically, colleges have been built around the teaching performed by the instructors and not the learning done by the students? Lecture halls have desks all facing front, bolted to the floor, physically reinforcing the idea that the professor is the center of teaching and learning. How would one decide whether instruction should be around teaching or around learning? What is the answer? Only you have the answer in your heart.

	Often	Sometimes	Seldom
I learn best by listening to a presentation that includes presentation and discussion.			
I learn best by scanning written information followed by reading from a book.			
I learn best by writing down the information for subsequent review.			
I learn best by using hands-on activities such as models or posters.			
I understand when explanations are shown to me using diagrams and flow charts.			
I learn how the bicycle brakes work by taking the brakes apart and putting them back together.			
I always use graphs and charts in my visual presentations.			
I can tell the subtle difference between sounds when they are presented in pairs.			
I can drive from A to B by writing down the road directions several times.			
I can easily drive from A to B by following map directions.			
I usually get good grades in class by listening to lectures.			
When I think hard, I twirl a pen or pencils with my fingers.			
I prefer to spell a new word by repeating the word out loud rather than by writing it down.			
To get the same piece of information, I prefer reading a newspaper article to listening to a report.			
I like to chew gum or snack when I study for an examination.			
I like to form a mental picture in my head before I start sharing an idea with friends.			
I explain a multistep task best by using my fingers.			
I enjoy listening to a good speech rather than reading the same information from a newspaper.			
I enjoy working with jigsaw puzzles.			
I twiddle objects in my fingers when I solve a mathematics equation.			
I prefer listening to the radio rather than reading the local news in the newspaper.			
I prefer learning information about the impact of global warming by reading about it.			
I prefer oral directions over written directions.			

Table 2.3. Learning Style Tally

SUMMARY AND REFLECTION

The course syllabus is a written educational contract or agreement between the professor and the students regarding teaching and learning. The construction of the agreement needs to be accurate to avoid unneeded challenges and problems. Knowing the students and himself well, the professor ensures effective teaching and learning. The classroom and the office are two extrinsic factors impacting the work environment of the professor.

Answer the following question as a form of self-evaluation: What do you need to know and do about the following to get yourself ready for the first day of class?

1. the syllabus;
2. the students;
3. the classroom and the office;
4. your own teaching/learning style.

REFERENCE

Gagliardi, Gary. *The Art of War: Plus the Ancient Chinese Revealed.* New York: Clearbridge, 2003.

Chapter Three

Probe into the Minds of Learning

Each new classroom of students is a unique challenge. In most disciplines, the make-up of the class always changes. There may be a wide span of student ages, in which outside commitments like work and family come into play. Maturity levels and how serious the student is about their studies can vary. Different ethnic and racial backgrounds add interest to the mix. Classes can be "quiet" or "too conversational." The professor must quickly analyze and adapt in the first class session or two, so that the class is vibrant to meet the learning needs of the students.

—Julie Davis

ANTICIPATORY QUESTIONS

- How does the change in demography impact the learning needs of the students?
- How does the change in learning needs impact the effectiveness of instructional strategies?

Dr. Owen is a newly appointed professor of a four-year public university teaching Geology 107. She has five years of experience teaching science in a local high school. Geology 107 is a science elective course in the undergraduate degree program.

She studies her class roster before the first day of class and she has twenty-seven students. The roster describes the class size and the mix of male and female students. What other student information can she assume? Can she assume that they are traditional full-time students in their early twenties? That they are from middle- or upper-middle-class families since the university is located in a prestigious high-end neighborhood? The assumption is based on Dr. Owen's prior knowledge when she attended college some time ago. The reality of the matter is that no assumptions can be made because the U.S. population composition has shifted in many different ways in the past 20 years. In the 20 years since 1980, the white population decreased 16 percent, the black population remained at about 12 percent, the Hispanic population jumped 10 percent, and the Asian population increased 3 percent (*USA Today*, 2012). Population diversity in the United States is on the rise.

CHANGING STUDENT DEMOGRAPHY

Let us examine three pieces of undergraduate student enrollment data from the U.S. Department of Education (U.S. Department of Education, 2009) to give us an idea about the general profile of the college students. The three pieces of data are age, socioeconomic status, and race/ethnicity. Age, socioeconomic status, and race/ethnicity are important because each is considered a factor of learning.

The first factor is age. The assumption about age is that it is used as a general assessment of life experience, much like how we divide the public school system into kindergarten through twelfth grade. In college, it is assumed that an adult student coming into the classroom has more life experience. Life experience brings a wealth of prior knowledge and perceptions about learning.

The data shows that the percentage of full-time undergraduate students enrolled in a public four-year college under the age of twenty-five is 49 percent, 24 percent for a community college, 21 percent for a private for-profit four-year college, 1 percent for a private not-for-profit two-year college, and 2 percent for a private for-profit two-year college (figure 3.1). Based on the definition of an adult as being twenty-five years old or older and the age data presented, one can conclude confidently that the majority of college students nowadays are adults. From the data, what can Dr. Owen assume about the age range of her students and the potential impact on learning and teaching?

The second factor is the socioeconomic status. The assumption about the socioeconomic status or the financial resources of the student is that it affects his chance of college admission and graduation. A college student with limited resources (i.e., below-average socioeconomic status) is likely to work a full- or part-time job to support his education. Otherwise, the student will not be able to afford a college that charges high tuition and fees.

Figure 3.2 shows the total percentage of full-time, first-time degree- or certificate-seeking undergraduate students participating in financial aid programs in public, not-for-profit, or for-profit colleges. The financial assistance programs can be one or a combination of federal grants (22 percent), state/

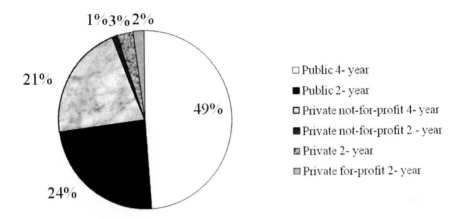

1% 3% 2%

21%

49%

24%

☐ Public 4- year
■ Public 2- year
☐ Private not-for-profit 4- year
■ Private not-for-profit 2 - year
▨ Private 2- year
▤ Private for-profit 2- year

Figure 3.1. Percentage distribution of students under 25 years old in the fall undergraduate enrollment in 2009 (source: U.S. Department of Education)

local grants (23 percent), institutional grants (22 percent), or student loans (33 percent) (figure 3.2). Another way of painting the socioeconomic status picture is that more than a quarter of the students need financial assistance to afford a college education. Based on the data, what can Dr. Owen assume about the resource needs of her students and the potential impact on learning and teaching?

The third factor is race/ethnicity. The assumption is that race/ethnicity brings in different values that influence learning beliefs and practices. For example, how does the student cherish the significance of education? How does the student construct knowledge? Does the student learn by rote memorization, by critical thinking, or problem solving, or a combination method?

Figure 3.3 shows the total percentage distribution of fall student enrollment in degree-granting institutions by race/ethnicity as 63 percent white, 14 percent black, 12 percent Hispanic, 7 percent Asian/Pacific Islander, 1 percent American Indian/Alaska Native, and 3 percent nonresident alien. The data varies among institutions that are public, not-for-profit, and for profit, and between degree-granting universities and community colleges.

In 2011–2012, the top three U.S. institutions of higher education with the most international doctoral students were the University of Southern California, the University of Illinois at Urbana–Champaign, and New York University (McMurtrie, 2012). Most of the recent growth in international enrollments has come from China, while the numbers from the other top-ten sending countries have remained virtually flat. The one exception is Saudi Arabia, where thousands of students have come to the United States on government scholarships.

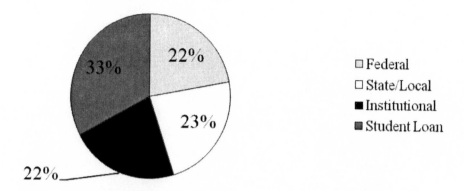

Figure 3.2.   Percentage of full-time, first-time degree/certificate-seeking under-graduate students participating in financial aid programs in 2006-07 (source: U.S. Department of Education)

Based on the student information, what can Dr. Owen assume about the race/ethnicity composition of her students and the potential impact on learning and teaching?

Age, socioeconomic status, and race/ethnicity are just the tip of the student demographic iceberg. Adult students are going or returning to college in record numbers. Many may have never attended college or may have started college and then stopped because of personal, financial, or other reasons. Some have spent time in the workforce, the military, or raising a family, and want to go back to fulfill lifelong dreams. Others want to update their professional skills and further career advancement. Still others are retired or are single parents looking to achieve a better life.

College students nowadays are, in general, adult learners. They are nontraditional in a sense that they come with different needs, they are motivated by self to learn, and they bring to the classroom a wealth and variety of life experience.

CHANGING TEACHING MODEL

The number of nontraditional adult college students is growing remarkably. Despite the change in student demography, it is questionable how many college professors seriously consider the impact of teaching adult students.

Education in the western hemisphere has long been influenced by the practices of the ancient world. The educational model of pedagogy came from a combination of the Greek words *paid* (to mean "child") and *agogus* (to mean "leading"). Therefore, putting the word parts together in *pedagogy* means "teaching children." The pedagogical assumption about learning was

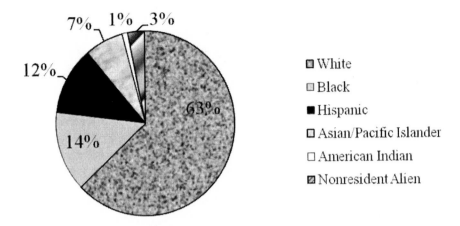

Figure 3.3. Percentage distribution of fall student enrollment in degree-granting institutions by race/ethnicity of fall 2008 (source: U.S. Department of Education)

based initially on the observations of teaching young children to read and write. It is argued that the pedagogy model is valid as long as the young student is building a foundation of learning. The model is later adopted and reinforced by didactic teaching. It focuses on the teacher's direct transmission of knowledge and skills to engage the student's mind. The didactic method of teaching is very teacher centered.

Shortly after World War II, there was a big influx of returning adults going back to schools. The pedagogical model of education met its challenge because adult learners seemed to respond to it as ineffective. Adult learners resisted the prescribed ways that knowledge and skills were transmitted. They appeared to learn in different ways. Knowledge gained is becoming dated within a matter of years. What people know today will become obsolete easily in just ten years. This is especially true in the area of technology. For that reason, merely transferring more knowledge to the adult learner is playing a game of catch-up.

Principles of Adult Learning

In the process of teaching adults, educators felt the need for a theoretical model of education different from pedagogy. They coined the word *andragogy*. It is from the Greek word *aner* to mean "man" or "adult." Welcome to the world of andragogy—education of the adult learners. The remaining chapter explores four scenarios to lay an intellectual foundation of andragogical principles to guide the learning and teaching in higher education.

Scenario #1

Sergei has owned a small construction business in town for many years. He was recently forced to close down the business because of the sluggish economy. Sergei decided to go back to school to earn an undergraduate degree in business to enhance his competency. He enrolled in an area university and he needed to take some foundation courses to satisfy his core program requirement.

Business 211 is a survey business course. The course surveys theories and principles in business. The semester evening class met once a week from 6:30 to 9:30 p.m. for sixteen weeks. The professor of Business 211 was a fresh Ph.D. from an Ivy League school. He determined what knowledge and/ or skills were to be learned, when they were to be learned, how they were to be learned, and if they had been learned successfully by the students. The course can be described as organized and structured, assuming the students to be dependent learners.

How does the Business 211 course meet the learning need of Sergei? After many years of work, Sergei is at a stage of his life that he is a less dependent learner and more secure in directing his own learning, although he might be still dependent in particular temporary situations. Sergei is an adult. He is an independent learner and the tightly structured class does not allow him to be flexible to be an independent learner. Sergei might ask himself the following questions about the course: (a) Is achieving the goal of the course of value to me? (b) What is the cost in terms of time and effort to reach the goal? (c) What is the chance of being a successful student in the class? The questions point at some value in the course for him and that he has a fair chance to succeed.

The first principle of adult learning states that adults have the psychological need to be generally self-directing. Learning is a dynamic change process, dependent on the self-efficacy of the learner to take responsibility for his own learning. It is therefore normal for an adult student to move from dependency toward increasing self-directedness and learning flexibility.

Scenario #2

Phoebe was a career mother with two children. She stayed out of the workforce for close to ten years to take care of her family. She earned her parttime living by taking care of her neighbors' toddlers in her own home. Last August, her youngest daughter started school when she turned seven. Phoebe took advantage of the time that the children were in school and registered in a neighborhood community college. She wanted to build on her passion of taking care of young children to become a state-certified daycare director.

Phoebe's first semester at the community college was a course in early childhood psychology. This was a core course requirement toward her certification. Mrs. Ferguson was the instructor of the course and she was a certified specialist in early childhood education. The course covered many aspects of understanding infants and toddlers and dealing with meeting their needs. A mid-semester assignment was a typed research report about the work of Lev Vygotsky in scaffolding children's learning. How would the research report enhance Phoebe's competency as an early childhood educator? Did Mrs. Ferguson assume Phoebe brought little to the classroom and that her experience as a daycare mother was of little worth?

The second principle of adult learning states that adults generally have a reservoir of experience that becomes an increasingly rich resource for learning—for themselves and for others. Adult learners can be a resource for their own learning and the learning of others. Therefore, adult learners attach more meaning to knowledge that they gain from experience than that acquired passively like reading from a textbook or listening to a lecture.

Scenario #3

Sean was a discharged military personnel. He joined the army right after high school and served six years in Afghanistan as an assistant reporter. Upon his return, he was interested in learning a trade and starting a family. He enrolled at a state university and pursued a career path in communication. He took Communication 250 as a core program requirement. Dr. Jackson was the professor of the course and his day job was a newspaper reporter with the *Chicago Sun Times*. Dr. Jackson's class used the textbook only as a resource and most of what he taught was from his own field experience.

Sean was motivated to learn and he felt the need. In contrast, many of Sean's classmates had undeclared majors, and they were not quite ready to be serious learners. What do you feel about the alignment of Sean's learning and Dr. Jackson's teaching? Would you expect Sean to achieve his career goal? Can you explain your answer?

The third principle of adult learning states that adults in general are ready to learn. They experience the need to learn in order to cope more satisfyingly with real-life goals. One example of a real-life goal is for an adult learner like Sean to go back to school to make a career transition. Adult learners are driven by an internal motivation to learn rather than some external influence based on the philosophy of "professor knows most and best" telling them what to learn.

Scenario #4

Sue was a veteran executive secretary of a church. Her main responsibilities were to assist the three church pastors in church communication and reporting. One month ago Raj, a church board member, recommended and donated a brand-new computer communication software program to the church. With the program, the church was supposed to improve its communication with the congregation. The challenge for Sue was to learn all the features of the new program and to maximize its application. She enrolled in a technology class at a local community college. The class was very specific about teaching a sample of communication software and the one that Sue wanted to learn was one of them.

Mr. Robertson was the course instructor. He was an information technology specialist of a big local company. His method of instruction had little theory. He would go into a specific software program, explain the overall features, and then go right into the application and practice of the features. What do you feel about the instructional method? Could it meet the learning needs of Sue or not? And why?

The fourth principle of adult learning states that adults in general see education as a process of developing increased competence to achieve their full potential in life. They want to apply whatever knowledge and skills they gain to living more productively tomorrow. In the classroom, there is a need for immediate application of theory to practice, thus emphasizing practical transitions of learning to the real world.

Andragogy is premised on four nonexclusive principles about the characteristics of adult learners. The first one says that the self-concept of the learner transitions from being dependent (i.e., in pedagogy) toward more independent learning. Second, adult learners bring with them a reservoir of experience versus limited experience (i.e., in pedagogy) that becomes an increasingly rich resource for learning. Third, adult learners are more ready to learn now than learning for the future (i.e., in pedagogy) to meet the goals that they set to improve their lives. Fourth, an adult's time perspective of learning is more immediacy of application than postponed application (i.e., in pedagogy).

THE ANDRAGOGY-PEDAGOGY CONTINUUM

At the beginning of the chapter, the age of college students according to the U.S. Department of Education was described and compared. The statistics show that about half of all college students are over the age of twenty-five in a four-year public university. The assumption leads to the premise that the remaining half is under the age of twenty-five. Based also on an earlier definition of *adult* as age twenty-five and older, one would expect a mix of adult and pre-adult students in a typical college class, say, in Dr. Owen's Geology 107 course.

Assuming a mix of adult and pre-adult students means that knowing the learning psychology of adult learners only will not help the professor to work effectively with all the students. In higher education, it is important to understand that andragogy and pedagogy are not two exclusive models of teaching. Rather, andragogy and pedagogy form a continuum.

Figure 3.4 describes the nature of the continuum. Inside the upper shaded triangle are the four traits of pre-adult learning discussed. The traits are dependent learning, limited learner experience, a need to learn, and learning as knowledge/skills acquisition. The four traits constitute the model of pedagogy. As one moves from the left-hand side (i.e., the broad base of the triangle) to the right-hand side (i.e., the apex of the triangle) of the shaded triangle, the learning traits diminish figuratively. The lower unshaded triangle is next. Inside the lower triangle are the four traits of adult learning. The traits are independent learning, rich learner experience, needs to learn, and learning as acquiring competencies. As one moves from the right-hand side (i.e., the broad base of the triangle) to the left-hand side (i.e., the apex of the triangle) of the triangle, the learning traits again diminish figuratively. The arrow at the bottom of figure 3.4 represents the chronological and theoretical progression of learning through age/time.

The left- and right-hand sides of figure 3.4 represent the trait extremes of pedagogy and andragogy. Realistically, the traits of any learner can fall rea-

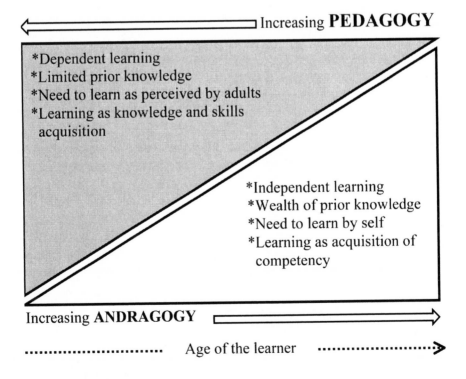

Increasing **PEDAGOGY**

*Dependent learning
*Limited prior knowledge
*Need to learn as perceived by adults
*Learning as knowledge and skills
  acquisition

*Independent learning
*Wealth of prior knowledge
*Need to learn by self
*Learning as acquisition of
  competency

Increasing **ANDRAGOGY**

Age of the learner

Figure 3.4. Pedagogy-Andragogy Continuum

sonably anywhere between the two extremes. As an illustration, if a student shows an equal mix of pre-adult and adult learning characteristics, then his profile of learning can theoretically be placed in the center of the pedagogy and andragogy continuum.

SUMMARY AND REFLECTION

It is a challenge to describe the general profile of a college student nowadays with reference to the age, the ethnicity, the socioeconomic status, and more. What is important to the professor is a good understanding of the learning needs of the students and how they learn so he may plan and deliver his instruction effectively.

Answer the following questions as a form of self-evaluation.

1. What are some major student demographic changes between when you attended college and what is in your college classroom now?
2. What were the major teaching styles of the professors when you attended college?
3. Do you feel that the same teaching style years ago will work in today's classroom? Please explain.
4. How does knowing that adult students (a) are self-directed learners, (b) possess a wealth of work experience, (c) are ready learners, and (d) are motivated to achieve a higher potential in life impact your planning and teaching strategies?

REFERENCES

Knowles, M. S. *The Modern Practice of Adult Education: Andragogy versus Pedagogy.* 8th ed. New York: Association Press, 1977.

Knowles, M. S. "My Farewell Address...Andragogy—No Panacea, No Ideology." *Training and Development Journal* 34, no. 8 (1980): 48–50.

McMurtrie, B. "China Continues to Drive Foreign-Student Growth in the United States." *Chronicle of Higher Education* 59, no. 12 (November 12, 2012). Accessed January 22, 2012. http://chronicle.com/article/China-Continues-to-Drive/135700.

USA Today, 2012 (Source: Analysis of census data by Barrett Lee, John Iceland, Gregory Sharp at Penn States's Department of Sociology and Population Research Institute.

Chapter Four

Enter the Stage (Environment) on the First Day of Class

The class environment in the first week is critical to allow the professor to give his first impression. The professor explores the best way he can about the students to get them engaged in learning. Likewise, the students test the environment to find if the class is a good fit.

—George Chakrabarty

ANTICIPATORY QUESTIONS

- What are the important things that need to be done on the first day of class?
- How do you do the important things well on the first days of class to thrive?

Like it or not, what you do the first week, especially on the first day, will determine your success for the rest of the school term. The first day is challenging because you are expected to hit the road running. You will start the class off with a number of nonteaching tasks and you are expected to perform immediately. Unfortunately, these tasks you did not learn in any of your previous formal or informal training. Welcome to the first day of teaching in college!

It is the first day of class. The classroom is a bit chaotic, buzzing with excitement, curiosity, and uncertainty. Despite how distracted students may look, they are actually paying attention. They want to learn about the course and the professor.

If you are not sure what to do on the first day, you do not have to figure out everything yourself. In this chapter you will learn from a to-do list. Do not feel overwhelmed. Choose the suggestions that enchant you much like your selection from the display of a delicious buffet table. In making your selection, keep in mind that college is a serious place for learning. It prepares students to grow to their fullest potential in business, education, computer, engineering, health care, languages and literature, liberal arts, technology, and other career choices. More importantly, you are one of the professors making it happen.

When you view the list of suggestions, you can ask yourself an honest question: Is this suggestion a fantasy, a tip for survival, a reinforcement of mastery, or an evidence of making student impact? Your answer to the question suggests your readiness to provide an adequate environment for learning and teaching. The fantasy, the survival, the mastery, and the impact are four successive levels of the teaching experience (Wong, 2009). The new professor may stage between fantasy and survival, while the veterans are secured between the mastery and impact level.

At the fantasy level of teaching, the professor believes a terminal degree in the field is the passport to success because college teaching is about dispensing knowledge. In addition, if he can relate well to students he considers that an added bonus. If you are at the fantasy stage of teaching, move on quickly.

At the survival level of teaching, the professor struggles to get through the day with ineffective practices. He complains about the work conditions and makes excuses for not doing a good job. The week-to-week survivor is likely to say something like, "This is college. I teach, and if students do not want to learn, that is not my fault." If you are at the survival stage of teaching, move on.

At the mastery level of teaching, the professor is on top of things. He manages the class well, expects much from his students, and teaches effectively. He teaches with enthusiasm and exhibits accountability. The master professor is likely to say something like, "I need to find a new strategy to help my students learn. I need to review and revise the class activities to make it fun and engaging." This may be a normal stop for many professors; however, there is always room for improvement.

At the impact level of teaching, the professor constantly looks for effective teaching methods. He bases his teaching on research-proven strategies, or has his own professional publication to impact the methods. At this level, the professor makes significant impact on student learning and he touches student success. A professor is both a teacher and a student. He teaches and at the same time learns to be a better teacher. He learns on his own, he learns from his colleagues, and most of all he learns from his students. The professor at this level of performance is likely to share his success with the college community and professional meetings. He can hold up to be a model of successful teaching.

With the background information about the different teaching levels, you can now study the suggestion list and decide what the best is for you. To develop an environment conducive for learning, the professor needs to give the class the impression that he is in charge by introducing himself, getting to know the students, explaining the syllabus, explaining the class routines, and beginning to teach to get the students engaged in the routine of learning.

Put yourself in the shoes of students. What would you like to know about the professor? Some students might already have an idea of what the professor is like by talking to students who had the class before. Your good reputation might draw many students to enroll in the class. On the other hand, a shaky reputation might steer students away unless the course is a core graduation requirement and you are the only person teaching it. Regardless of the perceived reputation, the professor needs to give students the first impression that he is in charge. The following is a list of tasks that the professor can do enthusiastically on the first day to introduce himself.

INTRODUCE YOURSELF AND TAKE CHARGE

1. Tell the students how you want to be addressed professionally. The options are Professor Brown, Dr. Brown, Mr./Mrs./Ms. Brown. It is a good idea to have your name already written on the board in case you have a long and challenging name to pronounce. Do not hesitate to say the name more than one time, especially if it is difficult to pronounce. After the brief introduction, the professor might want to move away from the front of the class.

2. Tell the students your formal training that leads to your teaching the course. Students are interested to know your professional preparation. It would be nice if you can share some personal old college photos. The idea is not so much to show off your young face but to share with students your personal college experience with interest and excitement.

3. Tell students about your professional accomplishments. Students often hear about their professor's accomplishments such as honor bestowed and articles/books published. Professional accomplishment indicates intellectual enthusiasm. If a professor has done research in the field, he is likely to give deeper perspectives in his inspirational teaching. Sharing your professional training, experience, and accomplishments inspires students about your transformation from a student to a scholar to now a professor.

4. Invite a former student to say something about the class. Have the student say a few words about his positive experience as well as challenges about the course. What did student evaluations say about your

class? If you have previous class evaluations, you can pull a sample to give students an idea and to remove any unnecessary student anxiety.

5. Pose yourself always as a professional. A professor might struggle to determine the relationship he wants with the students. He might be well liked for the following wrong reasons: he socializes well with the students, he does not care about real learning to prepare the students for the real world, or he is an easy grader. The right reasons for the students to like a professor are because he knows the subject matter, makes learning fun, helps students learn, grades papers promptly, treats everyone fairly, and gives purposeful and meaningful assignments.

GET TO KNOW THE STUDENTS

Next, the professor needs to know the students. This part of the first-day introduction includes the assumption that the class is not a large lecture hall with over a hundred students. Before the first day of class, the professor already has access to the class roster. For that reason, he should already know the class size, students' names, and student status with reference to freshman, sophomore, junior, and senior. The challenge for any professor is to learn the students' names as quickly as possible, like by the end of the first week. For the professor to call students by name is reinforcing the impression that he is in charge. Below is a list of strategies that he can select to get to know the students.

1. Learn all students' names quickly. Sketch out a classroom seating plan. Pass the seating plan around and ask students to write their names in the blanks provided (figure 4.1). Ask each student to say his or her name for you. Students do not like their names to be called incorrectly. Take a photo shot of the class with students in their respective seats. What does the professor have now? Names and faces that the professor can put visually together to get to learn the names of the students. Study the names until you can recall them by face recognition. You will be pleasantly surprised to see how the class will respond to you just because you recognize students' names.

2. Take a snapshot of the students' background. Beyond the basic student information of names, faces, and student status, one might want to know more about the students' prior knowledge about the subject, interests, career goals, and so on. This can be done by asking students to share the information on an index card. The professor may choose to share some of the information to give a snapshot about who are the other students in the class. The professor will be surprised to learn that

the information will later help him to understand the behavior and performance of students. For example, one would reasonably anticipate a student with a declared major to show more motivation as reflected in the class attendance and work quality.

3. Learn about the learning styles of students. Invite the students to take the learning-style inventory as described in chapter 2. The inventory summary score helps the professor to understand the student learning styles of visual, auditory, and tactile. This information is useful for appropriate lesson planning down the road.

4. Engage students to participate in a simple icebreaker activity. Here is an example: Ask each student to draw a shape on a blank piece of paper that best represents him or her. There are four shape options: a circle, a triangle, a square, and a wavy line. Allow students to think for a moment before drawing the shapes of their choice—what shape best represents them. Ask students drawing the circle, the triangle, the square, and the wavy line to stand up in turn. The number of circles, squares, and triangles should be about equal depending on the size of the group. The smallest group of students is anticipated to be the wavy line. The professor can then ask the students to divide into four groups so that each is a good mix of all the shapes. One personality interpretation of the shapes is that the circle people like to avoid conflicts, the triangle people often ask "what is the point?" in a conversation or discussion, the square people like to see things organized and tidy, and the wavy line people are creative and like to think outside the box. In the real world, we all have to work with people with different operational styles. These people are the circles, the triangles, the squares, and the wavy lines.

5. Defuse trouble-making students. It is unlikely that you will find trouble-making students on the first day. These students are immature, emotionally not stable, or some just out to make people's lives miserable. If these people are not dealt with quickly and fairly, the rest of the school term will be very long. Butting heads in class is not a good way to resolve the problem because negative encounters between the professor and the student are disturbing to the rest of the class. If a student has an issue, deal with him before or after class. Private dealings like that can save the face of both the student and the professor. Be specific about the undesirable behaviors and explain how that may harm the learning environment. Courteously ask what you can do to help him or her to adjust to the class better. Refer to the syllabus or the student handbook regarding expectations and consequences. Be professional even if the student is not. If you are not comfortable meeting with the student alone, hold the meeting in an administrator's office.

Why use icebreakers? If you are interested in creating a positive class atmosphere, helping students to relax, breaking down social barriers, or helping students to get to know one another, doing an icebreaker is recommended. You can access other icebreaker ideas in the library or on the Internet.

The introduction of the professor and getting to know the students are considered the informal portion of the first day. Keep in mind that if this part of the first day is dragged too long, the students will feel that the class is not into the serious academic business. Move on.

THE SYLLABUS

The syllabus is the roadmap of the course. It is the agreement between the university represented by the professor and the students and is a top official business of the first day. As a university employee, you are not supposed to teach only what you desire. The syllabus is the contractual guideline. Students need to be clear about the anticipatory set of the course and it is all in the syllabus. Here is a list of items that the professor can explain about the syllabus.

1. Do not read from the syllabus. It is not a good class-time investment and is often boring.

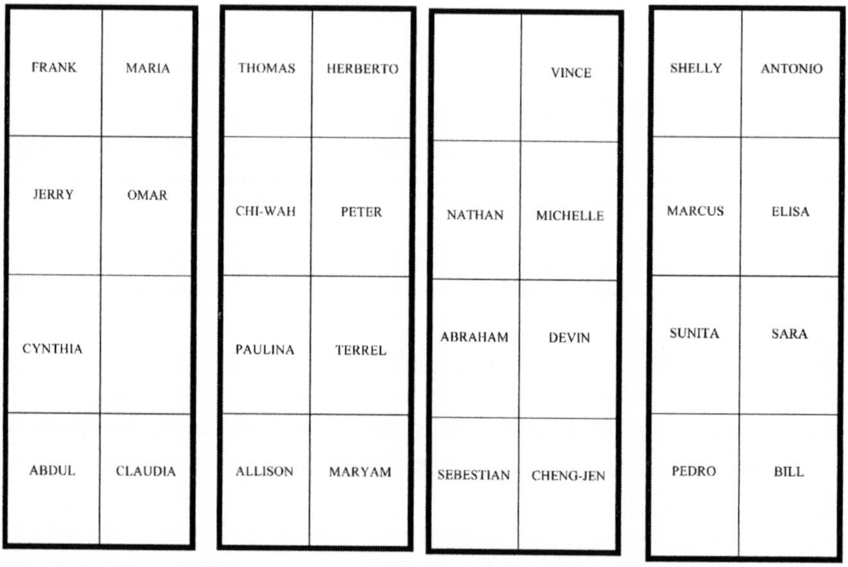

FRANK	MARIA	THOMAS	HERBERTO		VINCE	SHELLY	ANTONIO
JERRY	OMAR	CHI-WAH	PETER	NATHAN	MICHELLE	MARCUS	ELISA
CYNTHIA		PAULINA	TERREL	ABRAHAM	DEVIN	SUNITA	SARA
ABDUL	CLAUDIA	ALLISON	MARYAM	SEBASTIAN	CHENG-JEN	PEDRO	BILL

Figure 4.1.   Seating Chart

2. Paint a broad-stroke picture of the course by explaining succinctly the selection and organization of the topics in the syllabus. The syllabus shows organization, expectations, and preparation. The learners need to know the course framework for better broad conceptual understanding.

3. Summarize the syllabus by sections and highlight the importance. Pause after each section and invite questions. The process, however, can be reversed by asking the students to do the section summary. This way, the professor is setting the stage of engaging students' thinking and reinforces the collaborative philosophy of education.

4. Explain the grading system clearly. Students are always interested in the course expectations, the deliverables, and the grading guideline. To set a positive tone in the class, the professor can give students the confidence of being successful when going over the grading guideline. Some professors give students the option of taking a midterm examination or an accumulation of quizzes covering the same materials. What is the trade-off? Scoring a midterm is less time investment for the professor. Scoring quizzes takes more work for the professor but it is a lesser threat for the students and theoretically helps them to learn better. The selection of the options definitely aligns to the education philosophy of the instructor. Tell the students up front about the grading criteria—curve or no curve. Are the students graded on a curve, or are they graded against some pre-established criteria? One positive way to reinforce student success is by stating that every student starts the course with 100 percent or an equivalent of an A grade. Subsequent performance throughout the course determines whether the student can maintain the 100 percent or A. Starting with an A grade is setting high student expectations. It is similar to inviting students to drink from a full glass.

5. Walk through the teaching schedule. The ideal schedule includes the date, the topic of teaching, the corresponding text chapter, and the reading and/or class assignment due. Point out the breaks in the schedule such as spring break, winter break, public holidays, etc. Point out the not-to-be missed dates such as field trips, project presentations, the midterm, and the final examination. Above all, make students understand that the schedule is tentative to allow reasonable flexibility. Common sense says that the teaching, the learning activities, and the assessments must be well aligned.

6. Address the support services of special-needs students. Meeting the special learning needs of the students is legally important. Students with a documented learning, psychological, or physical disability may be eligible for reasonable academic accommodations or services. For example, some students may need the support of a note-taker, or an-

other person may need extra time to take a test. Make sure that the students know their rights and the support services for their needs; it is the law. In some universities, the support services are housed in the student services center or student success center.

THE CLASS ROUTINE

Next is the class routine. The class routine is one more nonteaching task that needs to be explained clearly on the first day of class. Routines that are not explained are subject to student interpretations. Unfortunately, some of the interpretations are nonproductive and even disruptive to teaching and learning.

Do you know how to handle student tardiness, chronic absenteeism, the use of communication devices, breaks, missing or late work, student participation, or questioning? Explain the set policy that is already on the syllabus or make one up on the spot. Issues in this area are not trivial pursuits. The professor will be challenged if there is no policy, and that means trouble. Do not assume that students will automatically take responsibility. It is always safe to assume that they do not.

THE FIRST TEACHING ACTIVITY

Now that the attitude of the students is adjusted, the professor can ease into teaching his first lesson. The first lesson you teach is not necessarily chapter 1 of the book. So what should you teach if it is not the first chapter? Regardless of the subject matter, the first lesson should include some of the following ingredients. Teach a lesson:

1. that is not too crazy, as you need to set the proper tone of the teaching-learning routine;
2. that does not require loading students with too much information;
3. to review some prior knowledge required of the course. Such a review lesson serves two purposes. It is an informal assessment of what students bring to the class, and it gives students the confidence of starting from their comfortable learning zone;
4. that is fun and exciting to whet the students' curiosity;
5. that has connections to the real world, or current affairs;
6. with several "activities," with the less desirable ones before the more desirable ones. The sequencing of the activities is a relativity theory of reinforcement like a parent asking the children to wash the dishes before watching TV.

SUMMARY AND REFLECTION

In conclusion, the first day of class should be one of high expectations, welcoming, and a celebration to give students the positive impression that the professor is passionate about teaching and the class environment is safe and stimulating for intellectual pursuit.

Please answer the following questions as a form of self-evaluation:

1. How would you introduce yourself to the students, and what elements in the introduction are important to the students?
2. What useful student information would you like to have, and how would you get it?
3. How do you explain the course syllabus to make it a binding teaching-learning contract?
4. What class routines are important to make your class run? How do you introduce and enforce the routines?
5. What is the lesson activity on the first day of class? What is your justification for teaching that lesson and activity?

REFERENCE

Wong, H. *The First Days of School: How to Be an Effective Teacher*. Mountainview, CA: Harry K. Wong Publications, 1998.

Chapter Five

Tackle the Core of Teaching—Knowledge

The successful professor must know the knowledge structure of the course and the critical elements that make them actionable for students.

—Ron Grevers

ANTICIPATORY QUESTIONS

- How does the professor make sense out of the knowledge that he teaches?
- Why is understanding the characteristics of the knowledge types important to effective teaching?

Ms. Beth is an education adjunct professor and she has been a state-certified public school teacher for over fifteen years. Last fall, she signed a contract to teach Education 605 at the university. Education 605 is a graduate course in education foundations and it is a required first-semester course for the Masters of Arts in Education program. As a veteran educator, Ms. Beth had no problems in sharing her school experience; nevertheless, a good portion of the course is based on a plethora of educational philosophies. Ms. Beth felt that even as a practitioner she still has a knowledge gap in that particular teaching area. Ms. Beth needs to understand the structure of knowledge to prepare her to teach the knowledge well. Ms. Beth is not unique in that she is a teacher and to keep up with the profession she also needs to be a student.

Regardless of whether the person is a teacher, a student, or something else, the person has to be on the move to pursue knowledge to sustain, and to move forward. In Ms. Beth's scenario, she has to acquire new knowledge (i.e., in educational philosophy) to prepare her for the new teaching assignment.

In order for Ms. Beth to find what she wants to know, she needs to understand what that knowledge is about so the acquisition of it can be on target. This is similar to saying that for a person to find an item he needs first to know what the item is. There are numerous dictionary definitions available but none are as easy to understand as a commonsense statement saying that knowledge is *the sum of what is known.* The statement is not technical and it points to two implications to mean that knowledge has parts (i.e., the sum is made of parts), and the parts together give it an identity (i.e., is known). Let us look at a knowledge model below to understand what knowledge is all about.

WHAT IS A MODEL OF KNOWLEDGE?

Knowledge is abstract and to render it more concrete we need to employ some analogies. The library is a place where people go to find information. A person finds the information from books, or from the computer. The library houses a large and organized collection of data, today typically in digital form. The data in the library are organized to model relevant aspects of reality such as the availability of rooms in a hotel. In a way, the data system supports processes requiring the information such as finding a hotel with vacant rooms. In a similar way, if one sees the library as a representation of knowledge, then we are close to seeing knowledge as being less abstract. The question remains about the ways the person retrieves the information from a large body of knowledge, discerning what is relevant and what is not.

That knowledge is *the sum of what is known* suggests that knowledge has parts, but how the parts relate to one another remains to be seen. Let us study a chemistry analogy. Scientists study the basic make-up of physical things around them and know that they are made of matter, which can be a solid, a liquid, or a gas. Matter is made of parts. The parts of matter (i.e., the sub-atomic particles of protons, neutrons, and electrons) are so small that they are invisible to the naked eye.

At the subatomic level, matter does not have an identity that people can recognize. A proton is a proton, a neutron is a neutron, and an electron is an electron. Nevertheless, when the subatomic particles are organized different-ly, the identity of the matter emerges. For example, hydrogen, a light and explosive gas, has one electron going around the atom nucleus of one proton and one neutron. Helium, a light and nonexplosive gas, has two electrons going around the center with the same one proton and one neutron nucleus. Here, the different properties of hydrogen and helium rest on the atomic structure of just one electron. As we move up the hierarchy of the atomic structure to the level of molecules, the identity of the matter gets even more complex. The fact is that some molecules react chemically with each other to form new molecules, thus forming new matter. Briefly, matter is made of parts and the configuration of the parts and how they relate to one another gives matter a wide array of properties.

Knowledge is similar in structure to matter in that it is made of parts and the parts work together differently in a hierarchical structure. A model of knowledge (figure 5.1) can be shaped like a pyramid. The base of the pyramid is laid on data that is raw and nonprocessed. Data can be a fact, a signal, or a symbol. In our daily activities, we come across many data that we perceive as irrelevant to what we do. The data is thus left alone and not processed. For example, when an office assistant works inside an office building, the weather data outside the building is not relevant to her work.

Moving up the knowledge pyramid to the next tier is information. Information is a collection of data that can be interpreted as a message. Information gives form to the mind (note: the Latin verb *informare* means "to give form") and it is organized data. Is the shaping of data to form information not similar to the shaping of the subatomic particles to form atoms? The information can in turn establish the base of discipline-specific knowledge. Knowledge is next.

Knowledge is a familiarity to include information of someone or something acquired through education or experience. Discipline-based knowledge

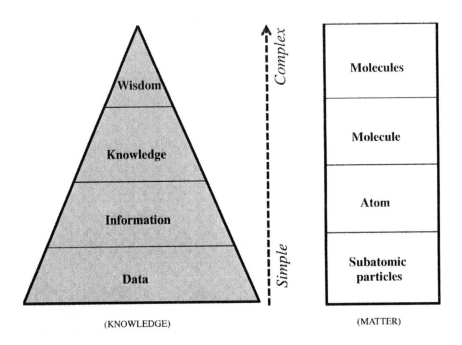

Figure 5.1.   A Knowledge Model

as in college teaching is specific in nature. Professionals in the area agree on a specific knowledge base for the discipline. Many people stay at the level of knowledge for a long time so they may get to do things right. It is through more experience (i.e., time) that the person may finally get to the apex of the knowledge pyramid to gain the wisdom of doing the right things.

In brief, information is defined in terms of data, knowledge in terms of information, and wisdom in terms of knowledge. In this respect, each level of the pyramid is seen to be a building block to the levels above. Understanding the structural hierarchy among data, information, knowledge, and wisdom is important when the professor desires to impart that effectively.

The pyramid discussed represents one type of knowledge. Realistically there are four basic types: content, procedural, conceptual, and metacognitive. Let us find out what each type is.

WHAT IS CONTENT KNOWLEDGE?

To teach students effectively according to the course syllabus, the professor needs to understand the structure of the subject matter so he can help students be successful. The professor also needs to see how knowledge connects across discipline and to the real world. This kind of understanding provides a foundation for pedagogical content knowledge.

Lee Shulman (Shulman, 1986) is credited with introducing the phrase *pedagogical content knowledge* and the importance of this knowledge to successful teaching. According to Shulman, the teacher needs to master the content knowledge to become effective. Content knowledge includes the structure of knowledge similar to what has been discussed in the model of knowledge.

Education 605 (discussed earlier) is a good example. To orient the teacher candidate properly, the candidate needs to have a broad understanding of such topics as educational philosophy, classroom management, learning psychology, curriculum, instruction, and assessment. Such topics collectively constitute a specific body of content knowledge for the education foundations course.

WHAT IS PROCEDURAL KNOWLEDGE?

Procedural knowledge is the type of knowledge someone has and demonstrates through the procedure of doing something. This knowledge is practical in nature. Procedural knowledge examples are knowledge of formal language or symbolic representations, rules, algorithms, and procedures. This is in contrast to content knowledge, which is a type of knowledge that indicates someone knows something. This knowledge can be abstract in nature.

In learning a language, the student learns the grammatical rules governing an expression (i.e., a phrase, a sentence, a paragraph) correctly. The nature of the rules is procedural. Examples of some language procedures are subject-verb agreement, the use of present, past, and future tense, and singular and plural forms.

When a person learned mathematics at the elementary level, he learned to follow mathematics procedures. These procedures according to the set rules help the person to find solutions to given problems. For example, people think of computation as addition, subtraction, multiplication, and division. At this point, the person may beg the question about what else is there in mathematics if it is just the learning of procedures that mathematicians call algorithms. The answer is there is a whole lot more to mathematics than just learning procedures. In a similar vein, if we think of cooking as no more than following cookbook recipes, we would miss the joy of cooking and cooking would be very boring.

WHAT IS CONCEPTUAL KNOWLEDGE?

When a student thinks in terms of a representation of ideas in a system with distinct relationships, the person is activating his conceptual knowledge. Concepts are groupings of ideas, attributes, and steps of a process in a meaningful fashion. When done properly, the concept serves as mental shorthand. Typically, conceptual knowledge is a more powerful knowledge tool than applying content or procedural knowledge in isolation. Logically, *the sum of what is known* is stronger and more powerful than the parts of what is known. There are at least five forms of concept knowledge for the practical purpose of teaching. They are:

1. *Concrete concept*—concrete concepts can be touched, seen, or heard by the senses. Teaching examples using a concrete concept include the solar system, the structure of an atom, the anatomy of a flower, tectonic plate movements, the properties of matter, and the biography of the U.S. presidents. In teaching, does the professor know the attributes and understand the contribution and relationships among the attributes of the topics taught or discussed?
2. *Abstract concept*—abstract concepts have no direct sensory input. To make an abstract concept more concrete, metaphor and analogy are employed. The use of the hierarchical organization of atoms and molecules to illustrate a similar structure in knowledge is an analogy. In teaching, does the professor use appropriate metaphors to explain a concept that is abstract to explain and a challenge to understand?

3. *Verbal concept*—verbal concepts are explained, interpreted, and elaborated with language. In the application of the verbal concept, the student uses his ability to talk about the features of the concept using his own words.

4. *Nonverbal concept*—nonverbal concepts are sometimes abstract in that they have to be visualized. The development and construction of a mental picture to help students to see the big picture of things is called visualization. Teaching examples using nonverbal concepts include explaining the theory of dual decoding of the senses, using the Punnet square for genetic crossing, the organizational chart of a company, and a chronological event in history.

5. *Process concept*—process concepts visualize a series of events. They represent the mechanism or the development of a topic such as protein synthesis, mitosis/meiosis, photosynthesis, and chemical reactions. In teaching, does the professor ask the students to commit the process discussed to memory, or does he use alternate methods to rote memorization of the steps?

WHAT IS METACOGNITIVE KNOWLEDGE?

Metacognition knows about knowing, or learns about learning. Metacognition knowledge takes different forms such as the right time to use a strategy and how to use it effectively to learn or to solve problems. If a student is to be effective, he must first know his own strengths and weaknesses in learning. This is called metacognitive knowledge. The wisdom of knowing oneself in performing well in the real world is universal. It crosses Plato in ancient Greece to Sun Tzu in ancient China. Secondly, the student needs to know how to self-regulate his own learning. This can be done by a reflection on action to engage the student further in a process of continuous learning. In teaching, what activities can the professor provide for the student to reflect on his learning so he may continue and improve? The metacognitive process equips the student to learn from his own experiences, rather than from formal teaching or knowledge transfer. In teaching, does the professor encourage the students to think on their own, or coerce them to go down a similar learning path?

Figure 5.2 sketches the four types of knowledge and their relationships. The single triangle and the single circle represent content and procedural knowledge respectively. When information is linked together, they form concepts. Figure 5.2 shows a content concept, a procedural concept, and a combination concept with content and procedure linked together. Finally, when a learner reflects on the development of his learning and assesses its strengths and weaknesses, it is metacognitive knowledge.

The description of the four types of knowledge helps the professor to critically assess the focus of his instruction. One would expect a course in fine arts to be more procedure-oriented than a course in English literature. On the other hand, a course in comparative philosophy will be more content-oriented than a course in mathematics. It is reasonable to assume that teaching any course has a good mix using the different types of knowledge.

Now that we have an understanding of the knowledge types, we need to concern ourselves with the *depth* of the knowledge. *Depth* is a relative term because it can be shallow or it can be deep. The expression, *it scratches only the surface*, means that the process is shallow. In teaching, the professor has the option of scratching (i.e., teaching) only the surface with low-level men-

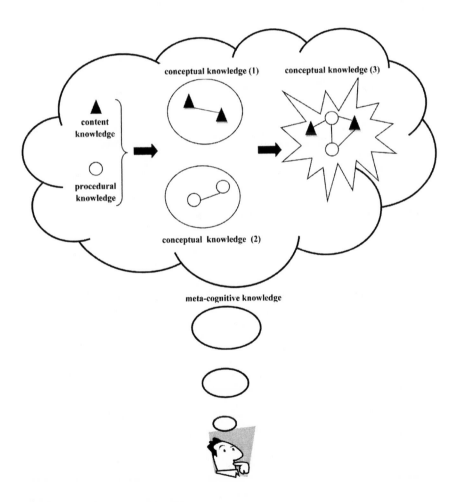

Figure 5.2. Types of Knowledge

tal activities (i.e., recall and recognition), or to go deep into the subject matter with higher-level mental activities (i.e., determine relationship, or make an evaluation).

Bloom's Taxonomy is a classification of learning objectives in education proposed in 1956 by a committee of educators chaired by Benjamin Bloom (Bloom et al., 1956). The original work of the Taxonomy was developed for three domains of learning: cognitive, affective, and psychomotor. Cognitive skills describe learning around knowledge; affective skills target the skills of feelings, emotion, and attitude; psychomotor skills describe the ability to handle a tool or instrument physically. In view of the traditional education skills of knowledge and following the interest of the knowledge discussion in the chapter, only the cognitive domain will be further explored.

The revised classification of Bloom's Taxonomy is a six-tier pyramid. Going from the base of the pyramid to the top are mental activities that are important to learning. The bottom tier is remembering, to be followed by understanding, applying, analyzing, evaluating, and creating at the top. The bottom three tiers are considered to be lower-level learning skills (i.e., remembering, understanding, and applying) and the upper three tiers are higher-level thinking skills (i.e., analyzing, evaluating, and creating). The place of applying in the middle tier of the pyramid is debated to be the hybrid between lower- and higher-level thinking skills, as it can be both.

What level of knowledge can the professor impart at each level of the taxonomy pyramid? If the teaching centers on knowledge recall or memorization, this is *remembering*; the lowest order of all mental activities. When the teaching goes to asking the student to explain ideas or concepts, this is *understanding*, the mental activity that is the next one up from the lowest. When teaching is about asking students to use knowledge in a new way, it is *applying*; the mental activity that is getting to the middle level of the taxonomy hierarchy. Asking the student to distinguish the different parts of an entity goes higher than applying. This is a mental activity that enters the higher-order thinking skill of *analyzing*. When the professor asks the student to make a stand or decision with justifications, the knowledge level enters the level of *evaluating*. Finally, asking the student to create a product or point of view is at the highest mental activity of *creating*.

In brief, the use of Bloom's Taxonomy reflects the depth of knowledge dealt with in the cognitive domain of learning. A decision regarding how to teach to the various levels of the subject matter is critical to the learning retention rate of students (figure 5.3). Shallow teaching with low mental activities has a low rate of learning retention and vice versa.

With what we learned about the four types of knowledge (i.e., content, procedure, concept, and metacognition) and the six levels of knowledge learning (i.e., remembering, understanding, applying, analyzing, evaluating, and creating) we now can go one more step to integrate the knowledge types

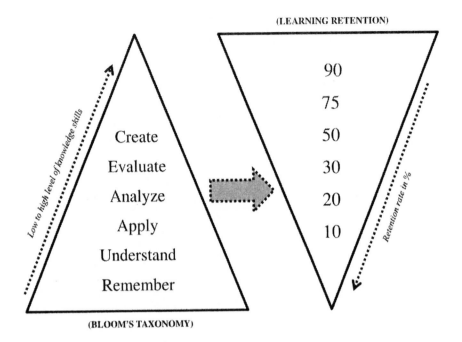

Figure 5.3.   Learning Retention Rates

and the knowledge levels together. Integrating the two sets presents the culmination of understanding knowledge in teaching.

Think about the two sets for one moment. What do they have in common? The common denominator is knowledge. This is similar to presenting the same thing in two different ways. Putting together the two in a four-by-six matrix will result in a grid (figure 5.4). The grid is made of two coordinates: the vertical (i.e., the y-axis of a graph) and the horizontal (i.e., the x-axis of the graph). On the vertical axis are the four types of knowledge, and on the horizontal axis are the six levels of knowledge learning.

The intersection of the axes indicates the specific identity of the knowledge type and level combined. There are twenty-four identity combinations. For example, cell number 1 is content/remember, cell number 2 is content/understand, cell number 15 is concept/apply, and the combinations continue.

Are you interested in finding out how you teach in the classroom? Use the knowledge grid as a score sheet. Have a colleague or students tally the type/level of knowledge you teach over time (i.e., a class period). What is the teaching pattern? Do you see a focus on a knowledge type that you want to impart, or a knowledge level that you intend to deliver? The score sheet is one concrete way to represent teaching information for the teacher to reflect on for metacognition!

LEVEL / TYPE	Remember	Understand	Apply	Analyze	Evaluate	Create
Content	1	2	3	4	5	6
Procedure	7	8	9	10	11	12
Concept	13	14	15	16	17	18
Meta-cognition	19	20	21	22	23	24

Figure 5.4. Knowledge Types and Levels Matrix

TEACHING SOME KNOWLEDGE THAT YOU ARE NOT FAMILIAR WITH!

Professors expect the teaching assignments to be in the range of their knowledge expertise. They have every right to stay with that expectation under most circumstances. Unfortunately, due to the recent economic downturn, professors are occasionally asked to teach in an area outside their comfort zone for the simple reason that there are just not enough faculty members to cover all the teaching areas. Is it not a dilemma when there is a gap between teaching as an expert versus teaching as a novice?

Teaching some knowledge that you are not familiar with occurs when the professor has to stand and deliver in front of a class and explain something that he just learned the week before, a day ago, or worse yet that same afternoon over lunch. Many people would take that as a stressful disadvantage. Did you know that situation can also work as an advantage?

The mind of a college professor needs to stay sharp by continuous learning and breaking into new knowledge territory. To teach an area that he is not familiar with encourages active learning and that is always healthy for the brain cells. When a person teaches a new area of knowledge, he honestly has a more realistic assessment of the time it will take a student to complete the learning task. Experts often unrealistically cram in more than what a learner can tackle. In addition, a person teaching a new subject is in a better position to relate challenging concepts of everyday, common knowledge to prior knowledge of the student because the novice instructor does not have a repertoire of specialized knowledge on the topic from which to draw. For all these reasons, the professor asking to teach a topic or even a course outside his area should count that not only as a learning curve but also as an opportunity to learn.

SUMMARY AND REFLECTION

Knowledge looks abstract, but it is not. Understanding the structure, the types, and the levels helps the professor integrate the application, the analysis, the evaluation, and the creation of it seamlessly for effective teaching.

Answer the following questions as a form of self-evaluation.

1. Compare what you need to teach (according to the course syllabus) to what you want to teach. Do you see a general agreement between the knowledge categories (i.e., content, procedural, conceptual, and metacognitive) of "need to teach" and "want to teach"?
2. How do you adjust the alignment between the knowledge categories between the "need to teach" and the "want to teach"?
3. Which category of knowledge are you most comfortable teaching, and why?
4. Which category of knowledge are you not comfortable teaching, and how can you ease yourself into the "uncomfortable" zone of teaching?

REFERENCES

Bloom, B. S., M. D. Engelhart, E. J. Furst, W. H. Hill, and D. R. Krathwohl. *Taxonomy of Educational Objectives: The Classification of Educational Goals; Handbook I: Cognitive Domain.* New York: Longmans, Green, 1956.

Shulman, L. "Those Who Understand: Knowledge Growth in Teaching." *Educational Researcher* 15, no. 2 (1986): 4–14.

Chapter Six

Unleash the Power of the Teaching Toolbox

Dr. Robinson's charisma and gifts of empathy made her a friend and confidant to many people at the university. She was a highly respected professional among colleagues. She passionately believed in the profession and would go the extra mile to support those gifts in her fellow faculty. Above all, Dr. Robinson was great fun. She had a box full of teaching tools and she used them with exceptional wit. All professors try to make their subject as inspiring as possible but few can make a lasting difference to a young person's life in the way that Dr. Robinson did for so many students at the school. It was enormously entertaining to be in Dr. Robinson's company and she will be sorely missed.

—Lori Wong

ANTICIPATORY QUESTIONS

- What are the tools of teaching?
- How do we use the teaching tools effectively?

Dr. Robinson took a retirement from teaching at the university so she could spend more time with her family. The description of Dr. Robinson above was a short speech by the department chair at the office retirement party. The audience learned a number of traits that can only be admired by Dr. Robinson's colleagues. If a faculty colleague can learn only one trait from Dr. Robinson, what would that be? It is hard to choose; is it not? Many pick being charismatic as important. Others pick the teaching toolbox also as important. This is easy to understand because if you look back on your own college days, when professors made learning fun (i.e., with charisma and various teaching strategies), you did not want to miss the class for anything.

SHOW YOUR CLASSROOM CHARISMA

If you want students to show interest in your class, one of the important tasks that you can do is to show passion for the subject matter. If you let your students see your enthusiasm, it will become contagious and vice versa. What made Dr. Robinson exceptional was her charisma. To be charismatic is not inherent; it can be cultivated every time you teach in the classroom from the first to the last day of the school term. It can be learned and it is on the priority list of effective instruction.

Choose from the following suggestions to cultivate your classroom charisma. Reinforce the ones that you are already doing. Do the ones that you are comfortable with before moving on to the ones that require more time and effort.

1. Smile. Bring your positive work emotion to class. Leave anything not conducive to work at the door. Students like a serious but not grouchy professor. To show that you are not grouchy (even if you are) put on a smiling face for the students. Being a smiling person wins half of the charisma battle. Remind yourself to pull up the corners of the lip as part of your professional demeanor.
2. Greet your students and call them by their names. You do not need to do that to every student in every class period as long as you do that consistently to eventually confer with everyone. Students feel a sense of belonging when they are recognized.
3. Be fair and consistent with the classroom routines. Students feel more comfortable if the learning environment is safe and predictable. It is interesting that students who know the routine will remind the professor if he forgets the routine, especially with break times and the end time of the class.
4. Laugh at yourself. This is one way to show that you, too, are human and you make mistakes (hopefully sometimes). A person who keeps defending his actions does not appear to be confident. How can you strike a balance with laughing at your mistakes and quibbling about your students making minor mistakes?
5. Stop doing annoying personal habits. Our idiosyncrasies are a part of us. Unfortunately, some small habits are annoying and distracting to the students. Poor eye contact and not speaking clearly are examples.
6. Stay in touch with students. You can stay in touch with students via class email especially when you meet only once a week with the class.

A good time to do that will be the end of the week like sending a Friday communiqué to highlight the assignment for the week and forecast the coming week.

7. Teach an engaging lesson. An engaging lesson is a two-way communication in the classroom. Avoid listening to hear only yourself and encourage students to share their points of view.

Rate yourself on the above suggestions. Are you already doing some? Give yourself a check. If you need to work on some, make a note. Be conscientious about those items that you need to improve and have another person that you trust help you do a follow-up assessment.

STATE THE LESSON OBJECTIVE

After an adjustment of charisma, the professor can now ease into teaching a formal lesson. Teaching is doing. In planning for teaching, the professor must translate the content or procedural knowledge into actionable or instructional objectives. Please note that if the objective is student-oriented, then it is more appropriate to call that "learning" than an "instructional objective." The instructional objectives are purposeful learning outcomes. Clear objectives help the professors to design learning activities and choose appropriate delivery methods. They make clear to both the professor and the students the expectations of the lesson.

Two elements are critical in the development of instructional objectives. The elements are the desired learning behaviors and the conditions of learning.

The first element, learning behavior, pinpoints the specific performance that is expected of students. The specific performance is intended to show understanding. Some words useful in writing cognitive objectives to show understanding are *classify*, *interpret*, *explain*, and *analyze*. In education, these action words are specific and they are measurable. In comparison, words like *understand*, *do*, and *remember* are not used because they are vague and hard to measure. One example of a geology instructional objective with specified student performance is: "The student will be able to classify rocks into the igneous, sedimentary, metamorphic groups based on their common properties."

The second element of an instructional objective is the condition of learning. The conditions for an instructional objective identify what the learner will have access to in order to demonstrate the expected performance. To elaborate on the previous instructional objective in geology, it will now read: "By the end of the rock unit, and given the fifteen rock samples, the student will be able to classify rocks into the igneous, sedimentary, metamorphic groups based on their common properties." There are two conditions stated in this objective. They are the time (i.e., the end of the rock unit) and the materials used (fifteen rock samples).

There are four knowledge types and six complexity levels that an instructional objective can be based on. According to chapter 5, the four types are content, procedural, conceptual, and metacognitive knowledge. The six levels of complexity are remembering, understanding, applying, analyzing, evaluating, and creating.

If you think that stating an instructional objective has no real purpose because you already know what you are planning to teach, think again. Is it not true that if you do not know where you are going, you might end up somewhere else? The objective statement if placed in a PowerPoint slide or written on the board is a visual reminder regarding the lesson's destination to keep both teaching and learning on task. A professor was in the middle of teaching a concept and got sidetracked by his own personal stories. She saw the objective that she wrote on the board and wound down the stories and went back quickly to the lesson agenda. In short, the objective helps you get a clearer picture of what you are doing with your lesson.

The instructional objectives should be written in such a way that they are:

1. general enough to be related to the broad goals of the syllabus, and specific enough to give clear direction regarding what the learner should do;
2. challenging yet attainable for the students;
3. appropriate for the subject matter; and
4. understandable for both teachers and students.

THE THREE LOGICS OF INSTRUCTION

A science professor once started a lesson by asking about the broad perception that the class has about the world around them. At the end of the introductory discussion, all came to the conclusion that the world is made of either matter or energy. With that base concept established, the professor carefully delved into the finer matter and energy categorizations with theories and examples. In a similar vein is it possible to identify a base concept for instruction in its lowest common denominator?

Intellectual activities are exercises of valid reasoning and it is assumed that teaching and learning, especially in higher education, involves logical reasoning. Logic is generally divided into three categories, and they are: deductive reasoning, inductive reasoning, and abductive reasoning. In short, instruction in a broad sense can be deductive, inductive, or abductive.

Deductive reasoning or deductive logic is the reasoning from one or more general known statements to arrive at a logical conclusion. Teaching the deductive method of delivery can be the elaboration of some wisdom as exemplified by rules, principles, or theories. A teaching manifestation is evident when a professor speaks knowledgeably about a topic derived from rules, theories, and principles. Deductive reasoning involves using given true premises or generalizations to reach a conclusion that is also true. For a professor to first define a principle in economics to be followed by examples is a deductive method of teaching. An example of deductive discussion can be: (a) staff retention is related to work conditions; (b) ABC coffee shop has a very high staff-retention rate; (c) therefore, ABC coffee shop has very good work conditions. One might even go further to find out the specific work conditions, including wage level, career progression, training, and the management.

Inductive reasoning runs the opposite to deductive reasoning. It derives general principles from specific observations. Inductive reasoning contrasts with deductive reasoning, in which specific examples are derived from general propositions. Dogs depend on air, food, and water to live. Cats depend on air, food, and water to live. Humans are living organisms like dogs and cats; therefore, humans depend on air, food, and water to live. Is this not the development of a general principle from two specific observations?

Abduction is a form of logic that goes from data description of something to a hypothesis that accounts for the reliable data and seeks to explain relevant evidence. Abductive logic can be interpreted as guessing a hypothetical explanation from an observation to surmise that something may be true. For example, the car parked on the street is wet. But if it rained last night, then it would be logical to assume that the car gets wet. Therefore, by abductive reasoning, the possibility that it rained last night is reasonable.

In summary, the three forms of reasoning commonly used in instruction are deduction, induction, and abduction. Deduction permits the derivation of B from A, assuming B is a formal consequence of A. Induction permits the derivation of B from A where A might give us a good reason to accept B. Abduction permits the inferring of A as an explanation of B. For that reason, abduction allows the precondition of A to be abducted from the consequence of B. As we explore the teaching toolbox further, you will find the use of the tools to be influenced by the three main logics of teaching.

EXPLORE THE TEACHING TOOLBOX

If a carpenter opens a toolbox and finds a hammer, the only job that he can do is to hammer or remove nails. With more tools in the box, the carpenter can perform more tasks. He can measure, cut, saw, smooth, glue, plaster, and paint, to name a few. The same situation applies to a professor in the classroom. If he knows how to lecture, he can only present a large body of information to the students with the predominant auditory mode of learning. In effective teaching, the professor may pick and change tools (i.e., strategies and resources) a few times during the instruction. The decision to select and use a particular teaching strategy assumes that it is the most effective, efficient, and appropriate means to facilitate learning.

Let us now open the teaching toolbox and examine the eight strategies of instruction. You may already have some tools in your teaching repertoire. Make sure that you know the function and limitation of each tool and add new tools to help you do a better job in the classroom.

Lecture-Based Teaching

Lecture is unarguably the most common college teaching method. It is used to present information to a group of students with the professor as the central focus of information transfer. Typically, very little interaction occurs between the instructor and the students during a lecture. Imagine yourself sitting in a large auditorium with more than one hundred other students in an American History 101 class. What are ways that the professor can teach and the students can learn? It is lecture.

A recent national survey (Berrett, 2012) of college professors reported that the lecture method of teaching remains the dominant form of instruction. Interestingly, this method of teaching has remained more popular among men than women.

The lecture method of teaching is familiar to most teachers simply because it was typically the way that they were taught. The method is straightforward to impart knowledge to students quickly. As the only dispenser of information, the professor has great control over what is being taught in the classroom. Logistically, a lecture is often easier to prepare than other methods of teaching.

There is one important consideration that the professor needs to consider when using the sage on the stage (or lecture) method. Is the purpose of the lecture method to impart content knowledge, procedural knowledge, or conceptual knowledge? Compare the three types of knowledge described in chapter 5 again. It is obvious that most lectures in general include a mix of the three. Nevertheless, what needs to be stressed is that conceptual knowledge is a high-level organization subsuming both the content and the procedural knowledge.

Students with learning styles other than auditory will face the challenge of not being engaged by lectures. Students may feel a lack of learning ownership because they are seldom given the chance to participate. Unfortunately, if the lecture method is perceived as a one-way communication method, the professor will never get a real feel of how much students understood and learned.

Many professors start the class with the large group (i.e., lecture) before switching to other methods of instruction explained below. Therefore, the lecture method is still considered the main item of the teaching toolbox.

Interactive Lecture-Based Teaching

Research says that the attention span of an average adult is about ten to fifteen minutes (Craig, 2009). This attention span can even be shorter if the students are easily distracted or not fully engaged. Honestly, beyond the attention span the mind tends to wander and will become distracted even by little things in the environment. Interactive lecture is a modified lecture with punctuated classroom activities. This way, a lecture lasting longer than twenty minutes will get a change of scenery to sustain student engagement. One purpose of the change of scenery is to use short activities to break up a lecture and return to the lecture smoothly. A guideline for the short activity is that it is not a replacement for the lecture. It is not a standalone strategy. What interactive activities can the professor use between the lecture segments? Let us find out.

Think-Pair-Share

Think-pair-share is one simple activity that can be used to divide up a long presentation. The activity can be couched against a backdrop of soliciting an application related to the lecture, seeking an assessment, asking for opinions, and so on. An open-ended question is likely to generate more discussion and higher-order thinking. An example question in economics can be, "In the context of the supply and demand model, what would be the effect of an increase in the minimum wage? Please explain your answer."

The purpose of think-pair-share is for the individual student to think about a question or issue alone before discussing it with another person (i.e., pair). The activity can be rendered more effective if each group is accountable for sharing with the class after the discussion, or if the professor promises to include the discussion content in the examinations. The professor can funnel all the small-group discussions into a whole class discussion and transition the discussion back to supporting the lecture.

Think-pair-share is a format change during a lecture using only a small amount of class time. It engages the entire class and often even engages nonparticipatory students. The student groupings can be fluid and the group membership can change also to vary the interaction dynamics.

Some think-pair-share activities are short; others are longer and more involved. The professor can use the student responses to vary the pacing of a lecture segment, and it is not difficult to employ more than one think-pair-share activity in a given lecture period.

Role-playing

Role-playing is another interactive lecture activity. It is an activity that applies knowledge in the role of decision makers. Similar to think-pair-share, this activity allows students to interact with fellow students as they try to complete the assigned task in the specific role that they play. Generally, students are more engaged as they attempt to personally respond to the issue from "playing" the role.

The challenge of role-playing is the design of a scenario relevant to the lecture material. It needs to include the different roles that the students play, information pertinent to the decision making specific to the role, and finally a task such as a recommendation to complete based on the information. An example in finance can be a scenario of a small business going through a budgetary reduction. How should the budget be prioritized if the business is to cut 15 percent? Each small group may include students playing three different roles: a mid-level manager, a staff member, and a clerk, for example. How do the different roles converge to a win-win decision?

Demonstration

Demonstration is a carefully prepared activity to visually expose the students to a visual understanding of a lecture concept. For example, the science professor may conduct an experiment in which the expensive equipment is not accessible to the individual students. The demonstration can also be a survey, or a simulation analysis of secondary data.

The professor's demonstration after a lecture is perceived as a secondary learning reinforcement of experience. It helps students to consolidate what they have learned before. When a demonstration is done with an unexpected outcome that is different from student expectations, it serves as a learning engagement and an invitation to learn. For example, a professor floats a six-pound bowling ball in an aquarium filled with water to dazzle the students. The students want to know why and the professor follows a lesson about the density of matter.

Field-Trip-Based Teaching

A field trip is an extended teaching activity usually done outside the classroom aimed at learning through observing, collecting, recording, and interpreting information. Fieldwork with students can be time consuming. The benefits, however, greatly outweigh the time needed to work out the details in advance and for follow-up.

Ask a critical question before planning a field trip. Does the field trip enhance and reinforce the course? Go ahead with the planning only if the answer is yes. A local museum has a special terra cotta warrior exhibit from ancient China. The exhibit includes a sample of archeological artifacts from the period. The field trip to see the exhibit is obviously the next best thing for archeology students to see the real dig many thousands miles away. Going on a field trip for the sake of going on a field trip, or any other reason, is never a good learning investment.

One logistical decision is selecting a field trip location. Where? Many outstanding field locations are either publicly or privately owned. Some examples are museums, arboretums, parks, theaters, libraries, and public offices, to name a few. Do you need to get a permit for admission? Is there a charge for the admission? Do you need to have a guided tour with the help of docents?

How much time is needed for the trip? Does the field trip occur during the class meeting, or is it an extension of the class on a weekend? One professor cancels a regular class and makes it up with a weekend field trip. It is obvious that for field trips some of the time will be used going to and from the field site. How to get there—transportation? Do you need to get a permission slip from students attending? Check carefully against the college policy.

Teaching with field labs is not lecturing in the field, or dropping off students at a museum and leaving them to their own devices. What are students supposed to learn? Define the learning objectives and the activities clearly before the trip. What are the student deliverables after the trip? Is it going to be a trip report of sorts?

Case-Based Teaching

In case-based teaching, students learn the work of the discipline firsthand, rather than reading accounts by other people. Students apply the concepts, techniques, and methods of the discipline and use their knowledge for application. Case discussions bring energy and excitement to the classroom, providing students with an opportunity to work with a range of real-world data, thus reinforcing what they have learned in the course.

Case study is a prevalent method of instruction in all areas and especially business courses. What purpose does a case study serve? A case study can be structured to serve a multitude of purposes. Most businesses and organizations use case studies to: (a) attract new clients by providing them with a means to identify with the case study client, (b) inform potential clients of the solution's benefits, (c) position the business or organization as knowledgeable about their former and future clients' challenges, (d) give all clients a background on the various solutions available, (e) overcome initial objections to their products or services, and (f) motivate potential clients to investigate further. In short, case study generates or tests hypotheses in a real-world context. It fits well into the deduction and induction modes of instruction.

Real-world cases using real-world data are usually messy and not organized like what students find in textbooks. The complexity of the problem requires students to use relevant information and screen out the irrelevant pieces, no matter how interesting they may look. Cases often have many parts and many points of view that require analysis, synthesis, and evaluation. The nature of the learning is at the higher level of the Bloom's Taxonomy of learning.

Case-based learning is motivating to students even when the material is challenging. Why? Students are active generators rather than passive recipients of knowledge. Students retain more from the experience than what they read from a secondary source of information such as the textbook.

Finding good cases is the ultimate challenge for doing case-based teaching. One can find good cases from professional journals and newspapers. The following are two examples.

Recycle or not? A Case from New York City. This case can be used in introductory or intermediate microeconomics courses. Externalities are among the important concepts covered in introductory economics courses. Therefore, the case can be used to reinforce the students' understanding of this concept through discussion and analysis of a real-world New York City example.

Too Many Deer? A Public Hearing. This is a case used in a biology class studying population dynamics. The case describes a deer overpopulation problem in two hundred plus acres of urban forest. The deer are causing vegetation damage. Different points of view are represented in the hearing. Here the students experience the reality of different opinions expressed and some have more merit than others.

Game-Based Teaching

Game playing is a popular culture for college students. They play games for relaxation, entertainment, and learning because they enjoy the engagement, the competition, and the immediate reward. If professors can design learning activities using the elements of playing games, students will eat them up quickly.

A game player likes to win. Many games have players working in teams to overcome obstacles or opponents as part of the game. Some games are addictive and often internal motivation is driven by curiosity, challenge, control, and fantasy. As soon as the game is finished the players get immediate feedback as winners or by earning points. We want games to be fun but more importantly they also need to be educational.

Many learning games are commercially produced. They vary from board games to activities that need assistive technology. It will take more than just subject-matter expertise to create a game-based lesson. In addition, the game requires visual support and artistic representation. The following are two examples.

Treasure Hunt is a generic game for many disciplines. The idea is to go to designated locations to find the needed information or object relevant to the assignment. A geology class may have students go to different sites on campus to look at the types of construction material (i.e., stone) of the building. After the collection of information, students can classify the materials and track their earth's origin. To make the game more sophisticated and assuming Global Positioning System (GPS) equipment is available, the treasure hunt locations can be purposely GPS defined.

Seed Germination is a computer simulation activity by Explorelearning.com. In the activity seed germination is affected by three variables: water, light, and temperature. By adjusting the three variables the grower can see seeds sprout with a click of the computer keyboard.

The activity can be tweaked into a game-based lesson. Students are given the task of seed germination. They have total control over creating the best conditions for seed growth by adjusting the variables. The person or the team with the highest percentage of seed germination is the champion grower and is the winner of the game. An additional piece to the game is the verification of results by data replication to produce the result. The lesson is good for teaching basic science, underscoring the application of the scientific method of investigation.

Discussion-Based Teaching

Discussion involves active student participation with guidance from the professor. Discussions build students' problem-solving skills more effectively than lectures do. However, fostering productive discussions are challenging for even the most experienced professors because starting a good discussion, sustaining the momentum, and finishing it with what is to be learned are the critical ingredients.

Starting off a purposeful discussion may rely on a previous reading assignment. Is the assignment serving the purpose the professor had hoped it would? It is obvious that discussions go better when specific references are made to an image, quote, event, scene, or moment. One strategy to prepare the start-off discussion is to give students the questions ahead of time.

The next day after the assignment, as students walk into the classroom, ask them to write down one or two items of discussion, thus soliciting input. Time permitting, the questions can be sorted into groups. During the class period, there might not be enough time to go through all the student questions. Therefore, the student questions can be drawn in a random fashion.

To sustain the discussion, the professor might have to probe with appropriate questions such as identifying the basic or common elements, compare and contrast, etc. Write the collective opinions on the board to provide a visual record. Some questions asked may be the pattern or relationships of the elements. The approach is clearly inductive to a generalization coming from specific pieces of information.

The format of the discussion may tweak into a forced debate in which students have to take sides and defend their point of view. "Are you for or against achieving racial balance in public schools?" "Capitalism or socialism in developing countries?" How do you deal appropriately with students who refuse to choose a side in a debate? Invite them to create a third group, thus creating a new dimension to the debate dynamics.

Be prepared to sum up the main points of the discussion and present it to the class as the "what have we learned?" moment. An alternative is to ask students to sum up the points for closure.

What has been presented thus far is preparing and conducting a class discussion with much structure and direction. The other option is to give students the opportunity to lead the discussion when the professor feels that he has been dominating the discussion. The professor can take notes on the side, and at the end of the session he can report the notes back to the students as a form of feedback.

Laboratory-Based Teaching

A laboratory is defined as a place of investigation. Students in the laboratory use equipment to conduct experiments to find information. The nature of laboratory-based teaching associates it more to teaching in the science disciplines. Laboratory-based teaching is generally an extension of the class lecture and is not designed to be a stand-alone teaching strategy.

Effective laboratory teaching requires both pedagogic and logistic decisions. Pedagogical decisions include deciding how to structure the laboratory session, what kinds of follow-up activities are appropriate, and how to help students work as individuals and in groups. Logistical decisions include deciding on the use of basic and specialized laboratory equipment.

It is possible that investigation can be done without the actual laboratory equipment. It is through computer-simulation laboratory experience (to be explained in chapter 8)

Concept-Based Teaching

A concept is bigger than an idea because it is an aggregate of small ideas. In geography, a point on a map is defined by the intersection of two imaginary line coordinates, the longitude and the latitude. To define a region, more than one point on the map is needed. Furthermore, the map points can be compared to other map points to determine the relationships. Similarly in teaching, the defined region is the concept and the map points are the small ideas.

Learning in any discipline can take the form of teaching small ideas such as facts. Ideas accumulate to form a cluster (i.e., concept) if they share common characteristics and exhibit relationships. Ideas that do not anchor to a cluster will soon be forgotten and not retained. Pedagogically, it is important to teach the facts. It is, however, more important to cluster facts to more stable cognitive structures called concepts. Concept formation is an effective way of teaching. It helps students to construct knowledge. A professor interested in developing and forming concepts is into concept-based teaching. The professor analyzes ideas and synthesizes them to form concepts. He can talk about a concept, or he can visually represent it using a map: a concept map.

A concept map is a diagram showing related ideas (figure 6.1). It is a graphical representation of knowledge: factual, procedural, or both. Ideas in a concept map are usually represented as boxes. The boxes are then connected with labeled arrows in a hierarchical structure from inclusive (e.g., wild animals) to less inclusive ideas (e.g., lions and tigers). The relationship between concepts can be articulated in linking phrases such as "can be," "results in," "is," "an example of," or "contributes to." The technique for visualizing these relationships among different ideas is called concept mapping. Concept mapping follows the following five steps.

1. Begin with a broad topic or question. For example, the success of first-year college students can be one. At the point of defining a topic, no details are required.
2. Brainstorm a list of ideas related to the topic. Related to the first-year college students can be class attendance, note taking, social life, financial support, hours of sleep, part-time employment if applicable, and so on.
3. Label and group ideas according to similarities. Ask questions regarding which of these ideas belong together, or if there is another way to group.
4. Regroup ideas if needed. This is a reflective process of fine-tuning the organization of ideas.
5. Connect the ideas and explain the relationships among the ideas. Linking phrases are used to explain and elaborate the relationships.

Figure 6.1 from a geology class describes the three major types of rocks as igneous, sedimentary, and metamorphic. The three types subdivide further into two to three categories ending with specific examples for each category. The layout of the map is hierarchical, with rocks at the top being the most inclusive and the fourteen rock examples (e.g., *pumice* on the left to *gneiss* on the right) as the least inclusive. Concept maps can be hand drawn or better still computer drawn. There are software programs that are designed to do concept maps and figure 6.1 is done by a mind-mapping software called *Inspiration 6*.

Concept maps are good instructional tools to demonstrate the cognitive structure of knowledge visually. Concept mapping is powerful if students are encouraged to develop their own concept maps based on the lecture to illustrate their understanding of knowledge. The power of concept mapping lies in the fact that the person (i.e., a student or the professor) constructing a concept decides what ideas go where in the map according to his own understanding. In other words, the person organizes his own understanding of a subject matter related to a concept. The process is very individualized.

Question-Based Teaching

Questioning is second to lecturing in popularity according to a study from the University of Southampton (www.pgce.soton.ac.uk/IT/Teaching/Questioning). Effective questioning serves to motivate students, evaluate students' performance, develop critical thinking skills, stimulate students to pursue knowledge on their own, nurture insights by exposing new relationships, and review and summarize previous learning. As a valuable teaching tool, questioning strategies will be described and explained more fully in chapter 7.

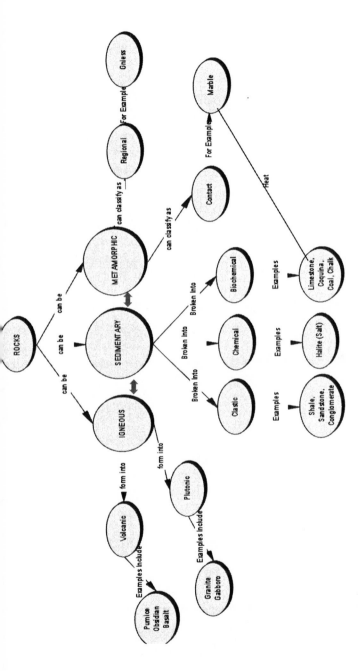

Figure 6.1. Rocks concept map

Chapter 6

A PEDAGOGICAL MODEL

How do professors organize the life of a class when there is such a wide variety of instructional options? Variety is the spice of life. The same truth applies also to the classroom when a variety of teaching strategies can stimulate teaching effectiveness and student achievement. Interestingly, researchers study the different exchanges between professors and students and come up with an insight into the general way many professors teach. Study and analyze the following exchange highlights between an education professor and his students.

The professor said, "Mr. Flintstone is a Paleolithic teacher from about 3.4 million years ago. Back in the Paleolithic (i.e., stone age) time, people lived a very hard life." The professor points to a picture slide on the screen and continued. "They have to scare saber tooth tigers with fire, catch fish with their bare hands, and kill wooly horses with clubs." The professor then fires off a list of questions: "What would Mr. Flintstone have taught the children back then? And what would have been in the stone-age school curriculum? As teacher candidates, what is worth knowing in your intended area of teaching?"

Students then offer a variety of answers regarding their ideas of what to teach and what a curriculum is about and proceed to the board to write down a list of teaching ideas that are worth knowing.

The professor then invites the students to the computer lab and explores learning goals and learning standards from the state board of education website. Students then get to compare their list of worth-knowing ideas to that of the state board of education. Students discuss the similarities and the differences, and the professor wraps up the lengthy discussion with the audience of learning, behavior of learning, conditions of learning, and degrees of learning performance as the ABCD of writing lesson objectives.

What is the general nature of the professor-student exchange? In essence, there are four phases. To start, the professor establishes and clarifies the common background of the lesson, which constitutes the academic structure. Have you seen a class where the professor is bombarded with unnecessary questions if the stage for instruction is not carefully prepared? Well-established academic structure invites curiosity and sets the stage of learning at the beginning of the class. Good academic structures let students know the objectives of the lesson and are a road map of where learning will take them. Review may be needed to help students to clarify prior learning.

LEARNING TO BE THE EFFECTIVE PROFESSOR

Do you recall your favorite professor you had in college? Do you recall what he or she was like? You might remember comments like, "He helped me understand the concept. The step-by-step process was very clear," "When I ran into a blockade, I felt like I could go up and talk about it with the professor," "I used to hate the subject, and the professor helped to give me the big picture so I could plug in the details," and "The professor made the subject come alive and I never had to look at the time!"

Only a very small percentage of professors are born with effective teaching traits. Look at the descriptions of your favorite professors. They practiced structure and clarity, motivation, high expectations, provocative questioning, and integrating preparation and theater. If you think that the best professors are born that way, think again. Professors tirelessly prepare and practice to perfect their trade of teaching.

SUMMARY AND REFLECTION

Make sure that the target of the lesson is clear to the students and stay on task. Be passionate about what you teach in the classroom from start to finish. Be creative about the tools that you select from the teaching toolbox, and remind yourself that the tool used has to fit the overall purpose of maximizing student learning.

Answer the following questions as a form of self-evaluation.

1. Assuming that you write an objective for each lesson, how faithful are you in teaching to the lesson objective?
2. If you are distracted from the lesson objective on a regular basis, what are your strategies for getting the lesson back on track?
3. What are the two tools that you use most in teaching? What is your justification for using those teaching tools?
4. What other tools do you feel can help you to do a better job teaching? How can you learn and use the new teaching tools in the near future?

REFERENCES

Berrett, D. "Today's Faculty: Stressed, Focused on Teaching, and Undeterred by Long Odds." *Chronicle of Higher Education* 59, no. 10 (2012).
Mellis, Craig M. "Optimizing Training: What Clinicians Have to Offer and How to Deliver It." *Paediatric Respiratory Reviews* 9, no. 2 (2008): 105–13.

Chapter Seven

Navigate through the Magic of Questioning

To question well is to teach well. In the skillful use of the question more than anything else lies the fine art of teaching; for in it we have the guide to clear and vivid ideas, and the quick spur to imagination, the stimulus to thought, the incentive to action.

—John Dewey

ANTICIPATORY QUESTIONS

- Why is questioning an important tool of teaching?
- How can questioning be used to stimulate effective learning?

Dr. Michelson is a professor of Astronomy 212. Students take the course because it satisfies a laboratory science requirement toward graduation. The science department chair one afternoon visits her class and notes the following classroom observation.

Dr. Michelson shared her deep and passionate knowledge about space science. The beginning of the lesson was about the vastness of space. She used different statistics such as 92,955,807,273 miles, 149,597,870,700 meters, 10,000 times the earth's radius, 930,000 hours or 106 years of driving (assuming a speed of 100 miles per hour), and the mean distance between the earth and the sun, etc., to describe the vast distance measurements in astronomy. Finally, after some twenty minutes of lecture, the concept of an astronomical unit was introduced.

Dr. Michelson asked soon after introducing the astronomical unit, "Does anyone have any questions?" There was complete silence. She waited, looked around the classroom, and continued with teaching the method of using the transits of Venus across the face of the sun as a method of defining the astronomical unit.

Telling is a mode of teaching and is common in lecture-based teaching and large-group instruction. There is definitely a place for teaching by telling, especially when the information is given for the first time. However, try putting yourself in the receiving end of a straight lecture. How will telling or plain giving information stimulate thinking and eventually learning?

What the science department chair saw in Astronomy 212 is typical. Dr. Michelson transitioned from lecture to question to make sure that she did not lose any students after the introduction lecture. However, the class silence should not be a surprise because only the brave students will venture out to ask questions.

How could Dr. Michelson have broken the silence after her question? For a quick fix, there are two suggestions. First, trade the general question with more specific questions: "What is the challenge facing the description of space distance with conventional measurement units such as miles or meters?" or "Describe the real-world connection of 92,955,807.273 miles, or 149,597,870,700 meters." A common instructional mistake made in the classroom is not the failure to provide the correct answer but the failure to ask the right question. Second, give students time to form small groups and come up with one or two questions. This strategy is useful when more difficult questions are raised. This way, the group questions overcome the reluctance of individual students because no student is put on the spot for asking "dumb" questions.

Can you see one gold nugget of wisdom from the Astronomy 212 experience? First, if not for Dr. Michelson's question, "Does anyone have any questions?" the teaching would have remained one long continuous lecture. Second, if there were no responses to the question, the teaching session would still have remained one continuous lecture. Do you see now that a valuable teaching tool available to the professor is strategic questioning? Good questioning is always at the very core of good teaching.

Questioning involves the students more in the teaching-learning dialogue. Unfortunately, many either fail to see what asking questions can do, or use it carelessly to promote effective learning. To question well means to teach well. The skillful use of questions brings out the fine art of teaching.

Astronomy 212 provides a limited view of a classroom. Ideally and theoretically, the professor and the students should both be players in the dynamic teaching-learning dialogue. Figure 7.1 describes the mind of the professor and the mind of the students connected by what they say (i.e., statements) and what they ask (i.e., questions) in the classroom.

Figure 7.1 compares two scenarios. Scenario 1 describes a classroom that is adult centered, as the professor gets to dominate the communication. The width of the arrows in the diagram represents the quantity of the communica-

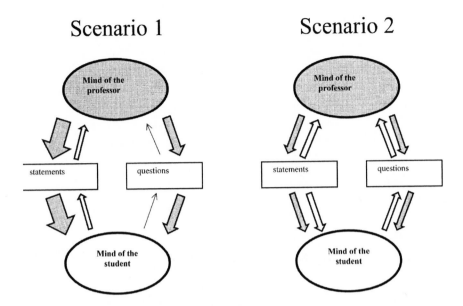

Figure 7.1. Mind Connections Between the Professor and the Students

tion. Lecture teaching is a good example of scenario 1. Scenario 2 describes a collaborative process with balanced inputs from the professor and the students. A debate or discussion session is an example of scenario 2. In teaching, it is imperative that students express themselves as active learners. It is, therefore, important to encourage students to ask questions and make comments.

Traditionally, questions have been used superficially to find out what has been learned, as seen in the assessment and evaluation of students' responses. Nevertheless, a deeper analytic approach of questioning goes beyond the responses to probe the reasoning behind them.

START WITH THE BASIC QUESTIONS

Since grade-school students are drilled with the five Ws (i.e., what, when, where, who, and why) and one H (i.e., how) as basic tools for asking questions to get information. Consider the following six questions: Who is it about? What happened? When did it take place? Where did it take place? Why did it happen? How did it happen? The wisdom of the questions is that each has an interrogative word that cannot be answered by a simple "yes" or "no." The five Ws and the one H were well remembered in Rudyard Kipling's *Just So Stories* (1902) in which a poem accompanying the tale of "The Elephant's Child" opens with:

> I keep six honest serving-men
> (They taught me all I knew);
> Their names are What and Why and When
> And How and Where and Who.

In questioning, there is no better place than to start with the basic five Ws and the one H. The question words *what, when, where, who, why,* and *how* are used to ask about specific qualities, quantities, people, times, places, and so on.

What?

What can be used as a standalone question, or it can be used in sequence questions. As a standalone question, *what* often asks for a noun response with reference to finding information about things or activities. What is the trend of the sequence of number? What is the major function of the enzyme protease in the reaction? What is the implicit message in the first paragraph of the article? The above questions request the person responding to remember, to recall some information that can be descriptive. In its simplest form the *what* question is a low-level cognitive process in Bloom's Taxonomy. You may refresh your knowledge of Bloom's Taxonomy in chapter 5.

The question word *what* may be asked in a sequence to make the cognitive process more complicated for problem-solving purposes. Examine the following question sequence: What is your career goal? What are the obstacles? What is your solution to overcoming the obstacles? To answer the questions, the information needs to be linked and cohesive. There are other uses of asking the question "What?" For example, if you ask, "You did what?" you actually are asking for a repetition or confirmation.

When?

When is a general question word asking about time. This can imply two different types of time. First, it can ask for a specific single time, or when an action will be completed, as in "When will you be finished downloading the iPad application?" Second, *when* may also ask a time duration or a time period, as in "When are you taking your sabbatical leave?" In its elementary form the *when* question is classified as a low-level cognitive process in Bloom's Taxonomy.

Where?

The question *where* seeks information about space, which can be geographic space (e.g., Chicago, London, Hong Kong) or regional space (e.g., Kindlon Hall, room 261). The English writer Rudyard Kipling wrote the well-known *Just So Stories*. Where was Kipling born? (Answer: Bombay, India.) In its elementary form the *where* question is classified as a low-level cognitive process in Bloom's Taxonomy. If something is happening, then asking "Where?" is a good companion question. Protein is made of amino acid molecules. Where are the amino acid molecules assembled in the cell? (Answer: Ribose Nucleic Acid in the cell cytoplasm.)

Who?

The question *who* brings people into the picture. The people are connected usually with actions, things, and places, as in famous people like writers, politicians, scientists, and other historical figures. For example, who is the first African American president of the United States? In many situations, stakeholders with an interest in the action or event are also included. The cabinet of the U.S. president is an example. In studying history, the knowledge of who (the person), what (the place), and when (the action) are the information that the historian needs to know well. In its elementary form the *who* question is classified as a low-level cognitive process in Bloom's Taxonomy.

Why?

Asking the *why* question seeks information of connection, relationships, and cause and effect. In teaching, a student may give a correct answer for the wrong reason. Because of that, the professor needs know the reason behind the student's explanation so he may gain a better understanding of the student's reasoning. Asking "Why?" seeks logical relationships and elicits the logic behind the thinking. In the teaching-learning dialogue, asking "Why?" is a good way to encourage a reflection of an assertive statement because the real "why" behind the statement might not be clear.

A reversal of asking the *why* question is to ask, "Why not?" Some years ago, a sociology professor asked a single critical question in the course's final examination. The question was, "Why sociology?" The question was meant to bring forth all comprehensive knowledge students had learned in the course. The professor expected to see pages after pages of answer. One student cleverly wrote the answer "Why not?" and received an A for the course. The professor later explained the two reasons for the A grade. First, the student through the course had earned enough points to get her an A even without taking the final. Second, the answer "Why not?" was a wonderful creative challenge to stimulate the person (i.e., the professor) reading the final to think outside the box.

In its elementary form the *why* question is classified as a high-level cognitive process in Bloom's Taxonomy.

How?

How means "in what way." *How* seeks verbs of process and is a probe for getting information about what has happened, what will happen. *How* is also a good probe for procedural knowledge regarding the process to get a task done. In this respect, asking the question "How?" is common in a science or technical project. In its elementary form the *how* question is a high-level cognitive process in Bloom's Taxonomy.

ASK A COMBINATION OF QUESTIONS

We have seen how questions of what, when, where, who, why, and how are asked individually. We have seen when the Ws and the H are used as stand-alone questions that many are classified as low-level cognition questions in Bloom's Taxonomy. Will the level of cognition be different if we use the interrogative words in a combination question? Let us find out.

Let us combine *what*, *why*, and *how* in the following sequence: What is the problem? Why is it happening? Can you solve the problem? How can the problem be tackled differently? Why did the solution fail/work the first time? What is next? These six questions provide a frame to problem solving. Problem solving is a high-level cognitive process that requires comprehension, analysis, synthesis, evaluation, and creation. Knowing how to skillfully use the process of questions to bring out the desired outcome is the ultimate art of questioning.

Using a combination of questions is important in teaching. Asking thoughtful questions helps the professor to distinguish what students understand from what students do not understand. Very often what a student understands is supported by his systematic thinking and what he does not understand is unorganized information from fragmented thinking. Using the technique of combining questions, the teacher is able to probe into the content, conceptual, and metacognitive knowledge of the learner.

Let us study the dialogue between a professor and his student in a life science laboratory.

Professor: Why are you using the dominant and recessive genes in the breeding?

Student: I am using both to see the phenotype of the F1 generation.

(The professor may ask other questions like, "How does your experiment relate to the class lecture?" "Why are you saying that?" and "Can you explain that to me in a different way?" The purpose of the questions is clarification. Asking clarification questions is similar to checking the reasoning behind the behavior of the learner.)

Professor: What is the assumption (or hypothesis) that you have before doing the genetic cross? Student: My assumption is that the dominant trait will appear in the offspring's phenotype.

(The professor may ask other questions such as" How can you verify your assumption?" "How did you choose the assumption?" and "How can you verify the assumption?" The purpose of the questions is probing for assumption. It is assumed that behaviors are based on hypotheses that we have. In this case, the assumption of the student comes from understanding Mendel's first law of genetics. Asking questions to probe students' assumptions is similar to checking the reasoning or logic behind the behavior of the learner.)

Professor: What would be an example of a dominant trait?

Student: It is the red eye of the fruit fly.

(The professor may ask other questions like, "If red is dominant, then what is the recessive trait?" "How can I be sure of what you are saying?" and "How do you know this?" Here the questions are based on investigating the reasons or evidence behind the action behavior of the learner. This is a good place where the professor may check to see if the student is giving the right answer but for the wrong reason.)

Professor: Is it possible that the eye color trait will mix with the shape of the wing trait?

Student: It is not possible because the traits are sorted independently according to Mendel's second law of independent assortment.

(The professor may ask other questions such as, "What is the counterargument for Mendel's second law?" "What alternative ways of looking at this are there?" and "What if you compare _____ and _____?" Here the questions are based on finding viewpoints and perspectives. Obviously viewpoints and perspectives have a significant impact on the behavior of the learner.)

Professor: How does the genetic experiment tie in with what we learned before?

Student: The experiment verifies the laws of genetics.

(The professor may also ask, "What generalizations can you make looking at the experiment data?" "What are the implications of _____?" and "Why is _____ important?" Here the questions are intended for implications and consequences. The ability to make a generalization statement requires critical thinking such as analysis and synthesis.)

Professor: Why do you think I asked all these questions?

Student: To make me think more about what I do and hopefully sharpen my way of thinking.

(The professor can also ask questions like, "Am I making sense?" "Why or why not?" and "What other questions might I ask?" Here we have a question about the questions. The learner needs to be reflective about a topic and how he learns, and this is a part of metacognition.)

In the above professor-student dialogue, six question types are revealed. They are (1) questions probing clarification, (2) questions probing assumption, (3) questions probing reasons/evidence, (4) questions probing viewpoints/perspectives (5) questions probing implications/consequences, and (6) questions probing the question. The six questions are designed to enhance critical thinking skills. Critical thinking is the process educators use to access, reflect on, and evaluate the reasoning behind our own and others' thinking and behavior.

In teaching, systematic and guided questions used to pursue concepts, logic, principles, issues, or problems are known as Socratic questions, named for the famous Greek philosopher Socrates (469–399 BC). The Socratic method of education in a nutshell is teaching by asking instead of teaching by telling. Socratic questions are not monopolized by the teacher. Socratic questioning also implies that students should be encouraged to explore, to consider reasons and evidence, to project forward to consider implications and consequences. Invite students to make up questions about a topic before it has been taught, promoting an atmosphere of inquiry.

ASK INTELLIGENT QUESTIONS

Professors as experts in their field are conscious about asking questions that are intelligent, or that appear to be intelligent. Now that we have established a base for the five Ws and the one H, we need to be critical about the critical elements of process and outcome to make questions intelligent. *Process* consists of perspective or evaluative questions. *Outcome* consists of knowledge and action questions. Here are some suggestions to reach the goal.

Ask a simple question in a context. How would your student answer the question "What is the common leadership trait of President Washington and President Lincoln?" It is always difficult to answer a question without a context. Asking something simple initially allows the students to know that you are about to explore something more complicated down the road. For example, "Who are the first and sixteenth presidents of the United States?" can be asked to place students in the question-and-answer mode. This can be followed by, "What are the presidents famous for, and why are they well liked?" After that you can make the questioning broad again and compare the two presidents. Here the question is simple, but you lay your general context on the table.

Define specifically what information is sought in the question. Do not be afraid to ask a question that you do not already have the answer for. Do not ask: "Can you tell me more about the icecap melt in the arctic?" Ask instead: "Scientists are saying that icecap melt is due to global warming, but others are saying that it is a part of the natural climate cycle. Can you explain which you think it is?"

Be professional and second-guess very carefully. Rephrase the question if you feel that the response to the question is not what you want. Proceed gently by asking how the student gets to know the information. This is similar to trying to understand the tools or logic used behind the answer.

Do not press the question if you feel the student is feeling uncomfortable and may be out of his element. As a professor, you are giving or seeking but not roasting for information. Back down and thank the student for trying when the answer is unsuccessful. How you handle wrong or "dumb" answers is a signal (positive or negative) to the rest of the class. Do not ridicule the student.

The process of handling answers is reciprocal for students asking questions. Encourage students to repeat, rephrase, and clarify the question if it is not clear the first time. Do not turn down a question and at the same time see that the question is not off-base. Some students may attempt to get attention by asking questions. Attend to those needs, or you may redirect the question to the class. Redirecting the questions around is a good tactic to get the class involved. Remember, being a polite and gracious professor is an important part of making the classroom conducive to learning.

Since questioning is key in stimulating learning, all students should have equal access to the opportunity for academic interaction. It is common that male students are asked more questions than female students. White students are asked more questions than nonwhite students. One of the reasons is that males are more assertive in getting attention, as they are more likely to call out answers to the questions. The other reason is that white students tend to be perceived as higher achievers than other racial groups and hence get called on more for questions. The bottom line is that the professors need to be fair and not just answer to the assertive and the squeaky-wheel students. The professor needs to establish rules and hold to the rules for class participation and questioning (see chapter 4).

WAIT TIME

Crystal is a first-year assistant professor. She gives an elaborate PowerPoint presentation about the process of animation in film making. She speaks very fast and with eloquence. She punctuates the presentation with questions. Many times she does not wait long enough and ends up answering the questions herself. Later she explains that teaching (including questioning) in a fast-paced manner is likely to be perceived by students as knowledgeable.

Crystal has her own idea about what good teaching is: fast-paced everything to include teaching and questioning. Here we want to tease out the time factor of questioning for discussion. A critical element of questioning is the wait time. Wait time is the length of time a teacher allows to elapse after the question is posed. For Crystal the wait time is less than one second. Is this a long enough time to elicit answers? In Crystal's case, students are more likely to be conditioned not to answer questions, knowing the professor will end up supplying the answer herself.

A wait time of less than one second is not long enough for students, particularly for those that experience difficulty in finding an answer. Studies show that for lower-level cognitive questions, a wait time of three seconds is most effective in terms of student achievement (Rowe, 1986). Shorter or longer wait times were less positively (within reason) correlated with student success.

For higher-level cognitive questions, the wait time can be longer than three seconds. Research has shown that students tend to be more engaged the longer the professor gives students to think. Increased wait time relates to significant student achievement to include higher retention, higher cognitive responses, longer responses, and more student-student interactions.

Equipped now with what we know about wait time, what can we suggest to Crystal to help her to engage her students more?

SUMMARY AND REFLECTION

Answer the following as a form of self-evaluation. In a typical class period:

1. How many questions do you ask?
2. How many lower-order questions do you ask?
3. How many higher-order questions do you ask?
4. How often do you answer your own questions?
5. How much wait time do you give?
6. How do you respond to students' questions?
7. How do you respond to students' questions if you do not know the answer?
8. How do you encourage students to raise questions?
9. What are some of the reasons that you ask questions?
10. Do you often pick certain students to answer questions?
11. How do you invite other students to respond to questions?
12. Based on the information gathered from the previous questions, do you have a plan for improvement, and what will that include?

REFERENCES

Dewey, J. *How We Think*. Revised ed. Boston: D.C. Heath, 1933.
Kipling, Rudyard. *Just So Stories*. New York: Doubleday, Page, 1907.
Rowe, Mary Budd. "Wait Time: Slowing Down May Be a Way of Speeding Up!" *Journal of Teacher Education* 37, no. 1 (1986): 43–50.

Chapter Eight

Integrate with Instructional Technology

If we are to see progress in student learning we have to integrate technology, pedagogy and change our way we deal with knowledge.

—Monique Woodward

ANTICIPATORY QUESTIONS

- What are the selection and application guidelines of instructional technology?
- How can instructional technology be used effectively to augment teaching?

Imagine yourself going back in time 150 years. Imagine yourself teaching in a classroom when electronic communication and information-storage devices were not available. What would you do as a teacher? You would have to depend on face-to-face communication with your students, describing, explaining with real objects, printed materials, and writing on chalkboards. You would hand-copy materials for yourself and your students. Teaching then was a very labor-intensive job.

Communication and information technologies increased by leaps and bounds when technologies moved quickly into the electronic age in the 1900s (figure 8.1). Videotapes, educational television, photocopiers, filmstrip projectors, hand-held calculators (later graphing calculators), machine test scoring, and computers of all sorts are just a selection of examples. Compare these technologies to the hornbook (note: the hornbook is a page containing the alphabets, or religious text covered with a piece of transparent horn or mica. It is fixed in a wood frame with a handle) used in 1650 (figure 8.1). It would be a challenge to even find the start of the comparison.

Later, as technologies entered the digital age, more tools were invented and used. In the late 1900s, computers were the centerpiece of technology study. Initially, educators had difficulties in understanding the role of computer use in the classroom until the late 1900s. In the 1980s the term *computer literacy* was frequently used in schools. The early notion of literacy is similar to learning *about* technology to include understanding the parts and functions of the computer like a machine. Later, *computer literacy* evolved to become learning *with* technology, as in educational technology such as using programming to teach specific skills of problem-solving.

The ease of computer use came around as the cumbersome DOS-based (note: DOS is the acronym for Disk Operating System of the IBM personal computer compatible market) systems changed to more user-friendly graphic-based interfaces with the Windows operating system and the Macintosh. In the late 1900s, computers were used more as communication tools to access information. The subsequent exponential growth of networked resources made information publicly available. Technology devices became smaller, faster, and more powerful. In this manner, the power of connecting the learner to the four corners of the globe was unleashed. What is important to note is that technologies have powerful implications for education and the failure to use these technological tools in teaching and learning today is not an option!

TECHNOLOGY-INTEGRATION EXPECTATIONS

Many college teachers nowadays are more technology prepared than ever before. A young physics visiting professor claims that he knows how to access resources, bring them into the classroom, and incorporate that into the presentation software to spice up the lectures. On the other hand, a veteran history professor with only limited technology tools at his fingertips disagrees. He argues that the quality of his lecture presentations is good if not better than his physics colleague because his students learn. Both professors have reasons to believe that they are effective with either much use or little use of instructional technology. However, how do we judge the reasonableness of the argument? Is the judgment based on the integration of technology in the classroom, the ultimate impact of technology on student learning? Which is the chicken and which is the egg?

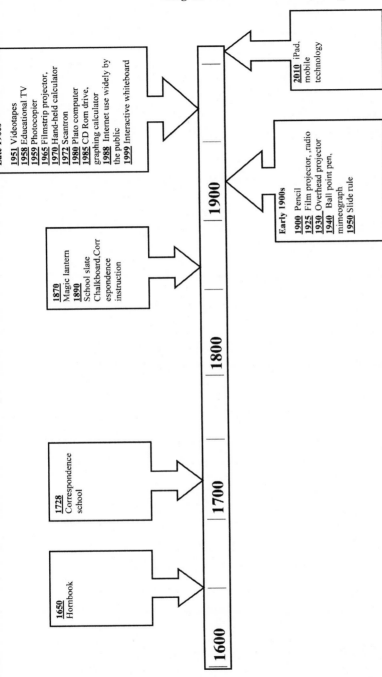

Figure 8.1.   Instructional Technology Timeline

An attempt to untangle the argument leads us to the common professional expectations of instructional technology, called standards. In simple terms, standards are criteria. Criteria define what is expected, much like the knowledge or skills that professors are expected to teach. These expectations relate to the performance of the individuals to include both the teachers and the students.

The International Society for Technology in Education (ISTE) developed five standards (www.iste.org) for instructors, and they are:

1. Facilitate student learning. Teachers use their expertise of the subject matter, teaching, and learning to facilitate experiences that promote student learning.
2. Design and develop digital-age learning experiences. Teachers design, develop, and evaluate learning experiences using contemporary tools and resources to maximize student learning.
3. Model digital-age work and learning. Teachers demonstrate knowledge and skills representative of an educational professional in a societal and global community.
4. Promote and model digital citizenship. Teachers demonstrate digital culture and show ethical behavior in professional practice.
5. Engage in professional growth. Teachers demonstrate effective use of digital tools and resources for continuous improvement of professional practices.

It is important to note that the ISTE has absolutely no authority to enforce the technology standards. Therefore if the institution that the professor works with has no mandatory compliance rule, then the standards will serve only as recommendations. Regardless of the requirements, the standards are important to guide the instructional practices in the classroom. The technology standards are:

1. provide a common set of expectations,
2. clarify the level of technological proficiency,
3. raise the awareness of what can be accomplished, and
4. focus the impact on student learning.

PRESENTATION TECHNOLOGY

To many college faculty members, media presentations, such as the use of Microsoft PowerPoint, are the norm of presentation technology. Veteran instructors in the classroom have gone a long way from writing on the board with chalk, to writing on the overhead projector with erasable marker, to now clicking and writing on the screen with a remote-control device.

Let us take the application of Microsoft PowerPoint as an example of instructional technology. How do we then go from good to better in Power-Point presentations? Here are three guidelines for the user:

1. Communicate the information succinctly.
2. Hold the attention of the viewers.
3. Stay on top of the presentation.

First and foremost, how do you communicate a message succinctly? How you present a piece of information can make a world of difference. Are the visuals clear, readable, precise, consistent, and professional looking? Use the slide masters and layout formatting, and you will be surprised to see the presentation going from basic to brilliant.

Take the time to outline the idea flow before making the slides. Is this not the same strategy that you use in effective teaching? The outline can be done easily by a slide title and bullet points of the main ideas. Use the slide sections in the latest PowerPoint version to help you divide up the presentation into logical segments for easier organization.

Use slide masters and layouts to get results. The built-in masters give the presenter a central place to add content. Formatting and layout changes automatically update all the slides in the presentation. For example, if you place your name and date on the slide master, it will appear on every single slide of the presentation. The slide master can be accessed by clicking on the *View* tab on the toolbar of the screen.

Secondly, how do you hold the attention of the viewers? Do the viewers have to read the entire slide to understand the message? Do not get into the trap of cluttering the slide with words and reading from it. Remember, if you use the right words, less is more. Use graphics on the slide to replace words. Select a chart or diagram to capture the essence of the information. For example, use a bar graph (which can be generated from Microsoft Excel) to show the profit growth of a company over time in lieu of a lengthy text narration. A well-picked chart or diagram can convey much more than boring bulleted text.

Augment the slide presentation with a theme (or title). A theme is a coordinated set of fonts, colors, and graphic effects that you can apply to the entire slide presentation. In PowerPoint you can apply the built-in theme with just a click on the *Design* tab of the horizontal toolbar on top of the screen. If a theme is not applied to the presentation, everything you place on the slide will not be consistent and coordinated, and that will certainly distract the attention of the viewers.

Punctuate the slides with short audio and video clips. In the recent edition of PowerPoint, you can insert a video that you have uploaded to a website to play directly in the presentation. There are many good websites for short video clips, and www.youtube.com has an excellent selection of videos from a wide variety of subjects. Add the built-in SmartArt graphics (in Office 2007 or later versions) to create professional quality diagrams such as simple lists or more complex process flow diagrams.

Use built-in animations to hammer the key points. Having text and graphics appear on the screen only when you need them is a nice touch to the presentation. Go to the *Animation* tab and find the custom animation pane.

Thirdly, how do you stay on top of the presentation? Use the PowerPoint features that are available to you. Theme, animations, slide masters, layout formatting, and SmartArt graphics are examples that have been described. Like any good presenter, preview the entire slide presentation to make sure that what you see is what you want the viewers to see. If external websites are used, pay attention to the connectivity. The unavailability of a website in the middle of a PowerPoint document will not only interfere with communication but also embarrass the presenter for bad control of the presentation. As an alternative, important video clips that rely on the external website can be prerecorded by video-capturing software to avoid the problem of poor connectivity.

College book publishers provide the instructor nowadays with a plethora of teaching tools to spice up the book deal. An instructor's resource CD typically includes a bank of test items, videos, and extensive chapter-by-chapter PowerPoint slides. It is not an exaggeration to describe the PowerPoint slides as extensive. For example, there might be over 100 slides for one book chapter. It will be a grave mistake if one plans to use all the slides to teach for one simple reason that nobody in the audience is likely to survive that many slides even if you break it up into several days. An overwhelming number of slides will clutter the communication process and drown the attention of the viewers. When you lose the audience, obviously you are not in control.

A simple remedy to the prepared-but-not-quite-usable slide situation is to be selective with what you have. Is this not similar to dining in an all-you-can-eat buffet restaurant? Be selective. Weed out slides that are not supportive to your teaching plan. Develop your own slides for customization and use the board to add your own illustrations and writing for personalization. Honestly, students love to see professors writing and drawing on the board to unfold the development of concepts. Too much of anything, even if it is good, needs to have a change of scenery and pace. Remember to have an appropriate mix of high and low technology teaching strategies to keep up with the learning interest and needs of the students.

SIMULATION LEARNING TECHNOLOGY

At the beginning of the chapter, instruction from 150 years ago is described as teaching using real objects and communication as face-to-face. In other words, the learning experience is direct with no mediation. Direct experiential learning is good. However, would it not be a challenge if the direct experience is not available, or if the cost of the experience is prohibitive? More critically, the instructor cannot perform a task endlessly just to get the essential concept across when he inevitably makes mistakes and fails along the way. Simulation learning is a viable option.

Is simulation learning better than direct experience learning? This question is often raised. The answer is an unequivocal "yes and no." Hands-on direct learning is always precious. Unfortunately, that type of learning can be costly and time prohibitive. This is where simulation learning is the answer. Simulation is instruction by design. Proponents of simulation learning would say that simulation is better because it compresses time and removes extraneous details to focus on the main learning event. Unlike real-world learning, simulations are designed especially to optimize learning.

Let us study three simulated learning examples, one from the National Geographic Society and the other two from ExploreLearning.

The National Geographic Society (NGS) is a good partner in education. The NGS has publications and websites that deliver high-quality educational information. For example, an interactive simulation website (www.nationalgeogrphic.com/forcesofnature/interactive/index.html?section=v) investigates the forces of nature to include tornadoes, hurricanes, volcanoes, and earthquakes. To study the forces of nature from direct experience even for professionals is too life threatening. Thanks to computer simulation, students can simulate an earthquake experiment by manipulating the variables such as the characteristics of the ground, the layout of the fault lines, and the intensity of the earthquake force. The NGS is one of the largest nonprofit scientific and educational institutions in the world. It offers many high-quality educational programs for audiences of all ages, and some of the programs are free of charge.

Would it not be nice if students could relive the legendary experience of Galileo more than 400 years ago from the top of the Leaning Tower of Pisa to study the behavior of free-falling objects? Unfortunately, there is no rewind button, and there is no turning back time. To relive the experience, students have to use simulated experience. Figure 8.2 is a representation of the experience where the experimenter can select and drop objects from the top of the tower and record the speed of the falling object. In the true spirit of learning, this simulation can be performed using a wide selection of variables relating to the falling objects and the experiment's conditions. ExploreLearning is the company behind this simulation program. It is different from National Geographic's program in that it is subscription based and not free.

Would it not be nice if students could work on mathematics problems at their own pace? For students ahead of the class they will be more motivated to learn if the instructor would allow them to move forward instead of holding them back for the rest of the class. For students who need time to work on the assignment, they would not feel embarrassed if the instructors would give them more time. The instructor is supposed to teach and accommodate the learning needs of all students. In education it is called differentiated instruction. Unfortunately, it is sometimes humanly impossible to run a simultaneous three-ring circus of differentiated instruction. Thanks to the advancement of learning technology, differentiated instruction is now more attainable than ever before. Let us study the following example.

Let us take a look at a simple college developmental math example of the slope calculation of a line. Figure 8.3 is the ExploreLearning representation of a simulated experience where the student can manipulate the four sliders on the left hand side of the screen to set the x and y coordinates of two different points. The graph at the right-hand side displays these two points and the line that passes through them.

When the *Show rise and run* option is checked or turned on, the student can move the x_1, x_2, y_1, and y_2 sliders left and right to see which one will

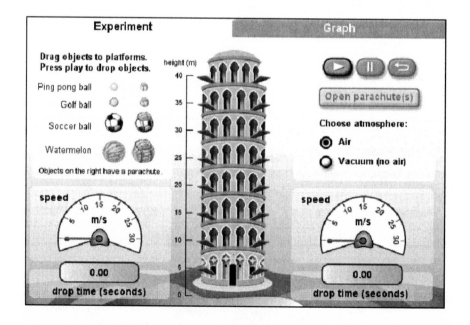

Figure 8.2.   Galileo Free Falling Object Experiment

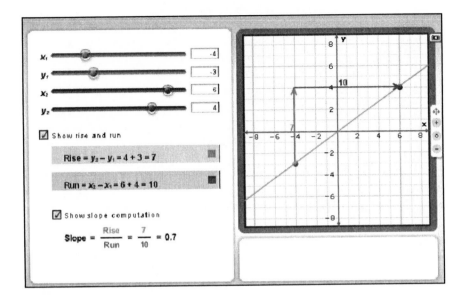

Figure 8.3.   Slope Computation Calculation

affect the rise. The student can also use the values of the sliders to find the rise between the two points shown on the graph. For other students, they may hand- or mentally compute the rise between any two points on a line without the use of the simulation activity. The student can next move the x_1, x_2, y_1, and y_2 sliders left and right to see which one will affect the run. Finally, the slope of a line is the ratio between rise and run. When the *Show slope computation* is checked or turned on, the student can see the visual computation of rise divided by run to give the slope.

The slope computation is an example to illustrate how presentation technology visually simulates the variables in finding and exploring the slope of a straight line. What is also important is that the computer simulation is able to accommodate the pace of different learners, thus leaving no one behind.

DISTANCE-LEARNING TECHNOLOGY

In 2007–2008 about 4.3 million students or 20 percent of all undergraduates took at least one distance education course. About 0.8 million or 4 percent of all undergraduates, took their entire program through distance education. The percentage of undergraduates who took any distance education courses rose from 16 percent in 2003–2004 to 20 percent in 2007–2008. In addition about 0.8 million or 22 percent of all post baccalaureate students took education courses in 2007–2008. The percentage of post baccalaureate students who took their program through distance education was higher than the percentage at the undergraduate level. (U.S. Department of Education, 2011)

In 2010, the University of Phoenix enrolled 307,965 students and Kaplan University enrolled 77,966 students. Arizona State University with a student enrollment of 70,440 students came in a distant third in enrollment ranking according to the 2010 U.S Department of Education (U.S. Department of Education, 2010). What do we learn from the given student enrollment information? The third-ranked Arizona State University is a public research university with its main campus in the Phoenix metropolitan area in Arizona. The second-ranked Kaplan University is a private, for-profit online university with ten campuses and learning centers in Iowa, Nebraska, Maryland, and Milwaukee. Finally, the top-ranked University of Phoenix is a private, for-profit online university with 204 campuses and learning centers. The main reason why Phoenix and Kaplan were able to enroll such a large number of students is because the two institutions are predominantly online universities, and course offerings are not restricted by any traditional brick-and-mortar structures.

The U.S. Department of Education reported a surge in the number of students taking online college courses (U.S. Department of Education, 2010), as seen in the quote. Why? To answer the question succinctly, we need to see both the needs of the students and the needs of the institution. Based on the fact that the majority of college students nowadays are adults, they need (1) more access to learning and (2) more flexibility in learning. Based on the fact that many colleges and universities are tuition driven they need (1) to increase the capacity of the educational program, (2) to increase the cost effectiveness of educational resources, and (3) to improve the quality of existing educational programs. In short, distance education meets the learning needs of the students and the educational and business needs of the institution.

The Business School at the University of Massachusetts at Amherst is an illustrative case study in the economics of distance learning. The bottom line is that the revenue generating from the distance-learning M.B.A. program has been profitable for the school. Twenty-six percent of the student enrollment at UMass's Isenberg School of Management is online, yet the distance-learning program generates about 40 percent of the school's $25 million annual budget (Blumenstyk, 2012). In other words, a smaller percentage of distance-learning students generate a large percentage of revenue for the school. How do they do that?

Distance learning is not bound by any brick-and-mortar structures, and it therefore has no physical space limitations. For that reason, the distance-learning program can enroll more students to generate more revenue. In addition, distance-learning programs can hire adjuncts to teach a curriculum for lower expenditures on the support services and learning-management system for distance-learning students.

What is *distance education* after all the foregoing introductions? It is learning when the learners are separated from the source of information by time or physical distance, or both. Presently, distance learning uses cutting-edge technologies such as satellite, computers, telephone, the Internet, and interactive video conferencing to enhance traditional ways of learning. Distance education ensures that more students have easier access to new and better learning than they had in the past, when they had to take only what was locally provided. For the simple reason that online programs are not restricted by time and physical distance, no wonder Phoenix and Kaplan are able to offer educational opportunities around the clock to boost the large numbers of students.

Is distance education new? The idea of learning from a distance is not new; however, the use of technology to enhance the process is what has been developed and advanced. The original idea of learning from a distance arrived in the early 1800s when courses of instruction were delivered by mail. Correspondence study facilitated learners to study from home or learners who wanted to study "independently."

In the early 1900s "schools of the air" were established by radio broadcasting. Radio mediated instructional programs were later displaced by educational television in the early 1900s. Distance education that emerged in the United States in the late 1900s was based on the technologies of teleconferencing and was a learning process that occurred in a class-like format. Finally, the application of computer networking for distance learning received a boost by the introduction of the World Wide Web. The historical root of distance learning is deeply rooted and the continuous technological evolution will only enable more and more sophisticated interaction between the learners and instructors.

Why is the understanding of system delivery of distance education important? Similar to a human body system or an engine system, distance education is a system with subsystems. The subsystems are the content, the course design, and the technology. The content is the knowledge and the principal source of the content knowledge is usually the faculty or staff of the institution. The course design is composed of the learning objectives, activities, and the layout of text and graphics. The technology is the computer with its browsers connected to the Internet, delivering text, audio, and video messages and means of interaction between the instructors and learners. It is desirable to have asynchronous or recorded technology suited to deliver content and synchronous technology for interactions between the instructors and the learners. Few instructors are experts in the three subsystems. For that reason, system delivery of distance education is the norm.

What is the general role of the instructor? In the system approach of distance education the production of an assignment by each student is a key component. In this case, each student completes and submits the assignment, similar to an e-mail attachment. The instructor reviews, gives feedback on, evaluates, and returns the assignment. In addition, sending the evaluation report to the administration of the institution is a part of the monitoring process. The instructor also facilitates the interactions of the students using technologies such as blogs or chat rooms. Here the instructors facilitate learning support and construction. When it is necessary to have an experience that cannot be simulated by technology, the instructor will have to plan and organize special face-to-face conferences.

What are the specific suggestions for distance-learning instructors? Model good online etiquette and make comments constructive and positive. Emphasize participation as an important part of learning and link it to course assignments and grades. Acknowledge student messages and regulate them to avoid cyberspace traffic jams. Control the number as well as the length of messages. Conduct online conferences by asking good questions (see chapter 7). The list of suggestions for online teaching continues. Keep in mind that effective online and on-the-ground teaching strategies are essentially similar; nevertheless, appropriate compensations need to be made to accommodate the mediated technology and the non-face-to-face communication between the students and the instructors.

What is the schedule format of teaching a distance-education course? Let us look at the Kaplan University requirements as an example. Online professors are required to hold two online office hours per week. They are to respond within 24 hours on weekdays and 48 hours on weekends when a student electronically contacts them. Weekly discussion boards are part of the class with a unit-related discussion topic required weekly for student/instructor interactions. In addition, scheduled sessions are also held online. Alternative assignments are made available to students who are not available for the scheduled session. Core classes include required weekly examinations that have to be completed within the weekly deadline.

What is the role of the online learner? To learn far away from a traditional classroom is oftentimes a challenge. As long as the learner has access to a computer, the place of learning can be at home, in the library, in the work office, or anywhere in between. To overcome the many distractions, the students must make a serious effort to have disciplined study habits.

Distance education opens up many new opportunities for learners regardless of age, gender, race, and learning interests. Beyond access, distance education gives the learners more control with reference to the institution of learning. We are already in the middle of a shift where the instructor is no longer the center of the education universe; the learner is. Teaching no longer drives learning; the learner does. Equally important is the learner side of the education equation. The learner needs to take more responsibility to manage their own learning to decide what he needs to learn and how much he learns, and finally he needs to assume the consequence of the responsibility. You may want to refresh and review the philosophical difference between an instructor-centered and a learner-centered classroom in chapter 2.

Faculty members who don't know the importance of distance learning in higher education or who are not comfortable in distance teaching miss a pivotal employment connection between them and their institution. As stated by the U.S Department of Education, the number of distance education students is on the rise and will continue to rise. Distance education is about a change in how students learn and how professors teach.

Melody Thompson (2011) coined the term *e-adjunct* to describe the unique role of online adjunct professors. Thompson also describes e-adjuncts as playing a broader role in the university experience than perhaps traditional adjuncts hired solely to teach specific courses. The e-adjunct ideally teaches and is involved in program development and evaluation, and is therefore more actively involved in the system delivery. Puzziferro and Sheldon (2011) suggest that e-adjuncts are particularly well-suited to perform in the competitive, student- or customer-oriented environment in which many higher education institutions exist today.

Do not be surprised when the hiring institution inquires if the professor candidates are able and willing to teach distance-education courses.

MOBILE TECHNOLOGY—THE IPAD

"We will not be using a print textbook this semester. Every student will study and read the electronic textbook using the iPad. You will also work with selected iPad applications (apps) to reinforce concept application throughout the course. Please come up so I may issue you your own iPad for the semester," announced Dr. David, a science professor, on the first day of class.

"That sounds very exciting because there is no need to lug around the big textbook anymore plus the iPad has access to games and music," said one student.

"I have heard about the iPad and I understand that it operates like my iPhone. I am excited because now I can access information a lot easier, and I am sure this will enhance my work productivity," said another student.

"I am an interactive learner and the iPad will help me to work smarter, so I may learn better and earn good grades in school," said yet another student.

Putting the classroom conversation pieces together gives the impression that the mobile device like the iPad is a tool for productivity, entertainment, relaxation, information, and applications that transcends all of the above. Understanding that the iPad opens the window to the world is important because of the significant implications it has for teaching. The many uses of the iPad may be compared to the well-known versatility tool the Swiss Army knife. Nevertheless, more important than the versatility of the iPad is the age-old question asking about instructional technology and its application effectiveness.

Educators using technology to boost the efficiency of the educational process is not new. When technology is integrated into meaningful and well-designed instructional activities, it drives student learning. We know that just having technology such as the iPad in the classroom is not as important as how educators use the technology to promote learning. For that reason, the first basis of using mobile technology such as the iPad is that the device has to enhance student learning, as the device itself is not the focus of learning. This rationale reinforces both the first and second standards of the ISTE, which we've already discussed.

Just because the first student says that the iPad is so much more portable than the big, thick textbook does not mean that learning will be enhanced unless an assumption is made that the student studies more now with the e-book on the iPad. Although using iPad games and music help with skill training like manual dexterity, listening, and calming down students, what assurance do instructors have that the students will not be distracted or isolated from the rest of the class? Unfortunately, they do not have any assurance of that unless the iPad is used in the context of supporting specific curriculum rather than allowing it to become an isolated instructional activity.

A good guideline for mobile device instruction is to engage students with explicit instruction, before inviting students to explore with curriculum-related apps, and encourage them to explain the issues or problems at hand before elaborating the concept discussed with purposeful "game" reinforcement. To end the instructional sequence with a game strengthens the fact that learning can be fun and helps finish the lesson on a positive note. This sequence of instructional events is similar to the phases of the learning cycle common to typical science instruction (Wong, 2008).

Another important basis of using mobile technology is that technology needs to be a part of classroom instruction because the future clearly requires proficiency in technological skills. This rationale supports ISTE standard number 3, discussed previously. As educators we know that the necessity of including technology in education-based activities is important to prepare students for careers from the counter at McDonald's to the executive desk of the corporate office. Consequently, maximizing the use of technology in instruction will provide opportunities for students to learn what they will use in future employment.

There are a number of mobile technology features that differ from other computers. For example, the device does not have a physical keyboard because it has an on-screen keyboard that automatically appears on the touch-screen. Tapping a text field in any application launches the on-screen keyboard. Although the keyboard is virtual, it has the same keys and has the same features as a regular keyboard. The iPad on-screen keyboard, for example, differs from a regular keyboard because it may automatically suggest words while you are typing depending on the application you are using. It is most interesting to watch how some students still use fingers to touch the computer screen right after their immediate and earlier use of the mobile device. The on-screen keyboard is here to stay and it may very well be the trend of future technology.

There are potential road blocks to the use of mobile instructional technology. The mobile device can be used as a demonstration tool, meaning that only the instructor has access and the rest of the class can just watch. Some lesson demonstrations are helpful if the experience is not easily accessible or is too expensive. However, in order to make a significant learning impact, students need to have access to the devices so that the interactive experience is personal.

To make mobile technology accessible to students is a big investment. In addition to the hardware costs are the professional development and the infrastructure support. The support behind the mobile technology is critical, like the continuous flow of electricity to a light bulb, where the bulb is the mobile device. Simply put, the cost of using instructional mobile technology effectively is more than just the cost of the devices.

There are other challenges. For example, iPad technology does not support *Adobe*, a popular video-streaming method on the Internet. For that reason, iPad users will be disappointed in the inability to access Adobe websites, which many educators use to support and augment instruction. Fortunately, iPad supports Youtube, which many educators fondly use to support instruction.

Mobile technology has comparable apps to Microsoft Word (such as Pages), Excel (such as Number), and PowerPoint (such as Keynote). A student may, for example, compose a written document, develop a spreadsheet, and create a PowerPoint using Pages, Number, and Keynote respectively. Mobile technology has no universal serial bus (USB) port nor compact disc (CD) drive, and input to the device in this respect is limited and, therefore, does not compare to a regular computer.

Regardless of what we think or say about iPad technology, we definitely need to hear it from the consumer—the student. Dr. David administered an online survey (Wong, 2012) to find out how the students liked or did not like using the iPad for the school semester. There was a forced-choice section and a free-response section to the survey. What follows is a summary of the forced-choice section.

Fifty-nine percent felt that it was easy to create content on the iPad. Sixty-eight percent felt that there were no issues with wireless access on campus.

Fifty-nine percent claimed that they used the iPad to access library resources. Twenty-seven percent tried to use the iPad to take class notes. Sixty-four percent recommended using an iPad as a primary means to access course materials. Fifty-five percent indicated that they would purchase an iPad if the device were used for at least one course per semester.

In the free-response section of the survey, students gave mixed responses about replacing traditional textbooks with e-books, as it would be a major reading and note-taking habit shift, though "it's easier to carry an iPad around" remained a strong reason for using the device. Students with a preference for using the iPad claimed that they were more interactive than traditional learners. Many students found more apps in the game and entertainment area than the CourseSmart, dictionary, or educational apps directly related to the course as they went further into the semester. Students explained why they preferred to use the iPad (e.g., academic learning for the course) and oftentimes gave the wrong reasons such as games and entertainment.

A way to describe the overall trend of the student response is mixed at best, with a leaning toward welcoming the use of iPad technology. The general student sentiment toward the iPad can best be described in the following comment: "I love this iPad. I want to be an iPad when I grow up, perhaps marry an iPod and start a family!"

One can comfortably say that the iPad, or another comparable mobile technology device, is the Swiss Army knife of education. That said, the Swiss Army knife only enhances and does not replace effective teaching by the instructor.

STUDENT RESPONSE SYSTEM (SRS)

Charlotte Danielson, an educational policy adviser and consultant, is renowned for her work in teacher effectiveness. The Danielson Framework is now the standard teacher framework in Illinois, New York City, and hundreds of institutions and districts around the nation. The Framework (Danielson, 2012) has four major domains. Specifically under the third domain (i.e., instruction) is the third component (i.e., 3c) of "Engaged Students in Learning." A benchmark description under the component says, "All students are actively engaged in the activities and assignments in their exploration of content." Danielson purposefully underscores student engagement as the critical element in successful teaching and learning. What, then, is the theory underpinning student engagement?

Engagement Theory (Shneiderman et al., 1995) is a conceptual framework that underscores the importance of students purposefully engaged in learning activities through interaction with others (to include the instructor) and worthwhile tasks. Wong reinforces and reconfigures the theory of engagement and uses it as the threshold to enter the learning spiral (Wong, 2008). While, in theory, learning engagement could occur without the use of technology, technology can facilitate engagement in ways that are difficult to achieve otherwise. Engagement Theory in the context of the current project proposal is intended to be a concept for technology-based learning and teaching.

Toward the end of chapter 6 a pedagogical model is described. The gist of the model is ideally a continuous dialogue between the students and the professor to ensure the critical element of student engagement. How can one sustain the ideal continuous communication if the professor uses primarily the lecture mode of teaching or when the class size is huge? Technology can come to the rescue. The professor can use a plethora of technological tools that in generic terms nowadays can be called the Student Response System, or SRS for short. In SRS there is still a big selection, and for the purpose of teaching and cost effectiveness, Poll Everywhere and Socrative will be discussed.

Poll Everywhere is cutting-edge web technology that replaces expensive proprietary audience-response hardware. It is an easy way to gather live responses in any venue: conferences, presentations, classrooms, radio, TV, print—anywhere. And because it works internationally with texting, web, or Twitter, its simplicity and flexibility are earning rave reviews. Can you imagine a professor standing in the pit of a large auditorium getting real-time electronic feedback from the students regarding a topic of the lecture presentation? Can you imagine viewing student opinions on a large flat screen for sharing and further discussion? Who says teaching is not interactive?

The best feature of Poll Everywhere is that it is free for audiences of forty people or less. Paid plans are available for larger audiences. K–12 and higher education semester-long plans are also available. You can access Poll Everywhere at www.polleverywhere.com and discover how it enhances teaching and learning instantaneously.

Socrative is a smart student response system that empowers teachers to engage their classrooms through a series of educational exercises and games via smartphones, laptops, and tablets. There is nothing that beats real-time feedback to determine if students really understand the lesson that you just conveyed. Professors have no clue what is really taking hold in students' brains, and this is where Socrative comes to the rescue.

Socrative allows the professor to pose a question and have students respond in real time. He can assess student understanding on the fly, and, best of all, students can use their portable communication devices to give near-instant feedback. The benefit of Socrative is that students do not have to buy a clicker device and the professor does not need to spend a lot of time developing quizzes using any certain format.

Socrative has two versions—a student version and an instructor version. Upon logging in, students enter a virtual room with a specified room number. The professors can see how many respondents are in the room and begin posing questions to the students. The different question options range from multiple choice, to true/false, to open-ended questions. Socrative compiles all the answers and presents them to the user on his screen or via email. If the professor uses an iPad to access Socrative, he can use it as a wireless mobile tablet and walk around the room with all the student responses in his hands.

Purposeful use of technology is very important in assisting learning. On the other hand, unplanned use is an invitation to possible distraction in the learning environment. That being said, finding a way to obtain feedback, using the feedback to create opportunities for expanded discussions, and having the feedback influence students' learning are some of the benefits of using tools such as Poll Everywhere and Socrative.

LOOK TO THE FUTURE

The future of technology in teaching is bright as long as it is used appropriately. The advancement of technology is faster than anyone's imagination. The three generations of iPad advancement in less than three years is a good testimony of extreme technology innovation over time. As an educator when you learn of another technological innovation tomorrow, what would be your response? You may say, "So what?" as you will not be able to keep up with whatever is the latest invention or development. But if you are fortunate enough to have access to the technology, ask instead, "What is the added value, and how can I integrate it to improve my teaching so student learning is enhanced?" Otherwise, from the educator's point of view the new innovation will have little value!

SUMMARY AND REFLECTION

In the world of instructional technology the medium is the message. Therefore, technology is not a neutral tool through which ideas flow simplistically from the professor to the students. Rather, the technology itself shapes those ideas in many different ways such as words, music, videos, and other forms of audio-visual images to stimulate the learners' experiences. The students already know that. It is just taking professors awhile to catch up. Integrating instructional technology means changing the traditional conception about learning and teaching. To be technologically competent or savvy means you can deliver what you teach in a manner that is more effective and fun to the learners. The application of instructional technology should not be intimidating. Attend professional workshops and conferences if you are not already interested in technology-mediated teaching, and you will change your teaching for the better.

REFERENCES

Blumenstyk, G. "One Business School Is Itself a Case Study in the Economics of Online Education." *Chronicle of Higher Education*, October 1, 2012. Accessed January 23, 2013. http://chronicle.com/article/Massive-Excitement-About/134668.

Danielson, C. "Observing Classroom Practice." *Educational Leadership* 70, no. 3 (2012).

Puzziferro, M., and K. Sheldon. "A Model for Developing High-Quality Online Courses: Integrating a System Approach with Learning Theory," *Journal of Asynchronous Learning Networks* 12, nos. 3–4 (2008).

Shneiderman, B., M. Alavi, K. Norman, and E. Borkowski. "Windows of Opportunity in Electronic Classrooms," *Communications of the ACM* 38, no. 11 (1995): 19–24.

Thompson, Melody. "Changing the Role of Adjunct Faculty in Online Professional Education." Penn State University, 2011. Accessed January 23, 2013. http://sloanconsortium.org/effective_practices/changing-role-adjunct-faculty-online-professional-education.

U.S. Department of Education, National Center for Education Statistics. *Digest of Education Statistics 2010* (NCES 2011-015). Accessed January 23, 2013. http://nces.ed.gov/pubs2011/2011015.pdf.

U.S. Department of Education, National Center for Education Statistics. *The Condition of Education 2011* (NCES 2011-033). Accessed January 23, 2013. http://nces.ed.gov/pubs2011/2011033.pdf.

Wong, O. "Revisiting the Learning Cycle and Its Implication to Science Instruction." *Spectrum* 34, no. 1 (2008): 26–32.

Wong, O. "Is the iPad the Swiss Army Knife for Science Education?" *Spectrum* 37, no. 3 (2012): 39.

Chapter Nine

Full-Circle Accountability

The professor evaluates the students and the students evaluate the professor.
This is the full circle accountability of college teaching.

—Henry Abdul

ANTICIPATORY QUESTIONS

- What are the methods of student assessment?
- How can the student assessment methods be used in a fair and consistent manner?
- Why is the assessment of students and professors important for the institution of higher education?

"Wondering which car manufacturers are the all-round best?" asks Dr. Berger curiously. He is a newly hired faculty member at the university and he is in the market to purchase a new vehicle.

"Why don't you consult the Automaker Report Cards by Consumer Reports? The publication is informative and I used it for my last car purchase," answers Dr. Greenberg, the department chair emeritus.

In two weeks, the two professors lunch again and the vehicle purchase makes its way back to the dining table conversation.

Dr. Berger says, "Four of the top five car makers are Japanese. There are no U.S. car manufacturers making the list. The top four are Honda, Subaru, Toyota, and Mazda. There is a four-way tie for fifth place and they are Mercedes-Benz, Nissan, Volkswagen, and BMW. It is disheartening not to see at least one U.S car manufacturer on top of the list!" Dr. Berger continues, "I wonder what the car top-five rating is based on."

"The ranking is quite scientific. It reflects the car's performance supported by road test data such as safety, fuel economy, comfort, and convenience. In addition, a sample size of over one million cars is tested," Dr. Greenberg answers. "It is most interesting because decades ago consumers were hesitant to buy anything Japanese," Dr. Greenberg continues.

Historians in the business world would not hesitate to explain the little-known fact that after World War II, Japan was seen as a nation with inferior products that no one wanted to buy. In a matter of half a decade, Japan turned around miraculously to lead the world's manufacturing market in cars and electronics. "Made in Japan" is now seen in the car-manufacturing world nowadays to represent quality products. What happened?

The secret to Japan's revival can be described in two simple words so many people in the manufacturing business are familiar with: *quality control.* The quality-control concept is best explained by the making of a car machine part. Let us say the specified width of the machine part is one centimeter. The U.S.-made piece will be one centimeter long, plus or minus one-eighth of a centimeter. On the other hand, the Japanese-made piece will be one centimeter long, plus or minus one-sixteenth of a centimeter. What is the big deal? While the two car machine parts are made to the same specification with an acceptable level of tolerance, the Japanese-made part makes the car run smoother with fewer problems and therefore gets greater consumer satisfaction. That is a big deal in manufacturing with a higher level of quality control.

While there are a number of quality-control theories, the best-known one was developed by Dr. Edward Deming, a statistician. Dr. Deming's quality-control theory is extensive. Relevant to the current chapter of full-circle evaluation is the principle of "drive out the fear." What is the "drive out the fear" principle?

Dr. Deming emphatically believes that only through effective communication without retaliation will the organization move toward improvement. Furthermore, through the "drive out the fear" type of communication comes slowly but surely the reciprocal evaluation between workers and supervisors. In fact, that was what transformed the Japanese manufacturing business from inferior to superior. In the spirit of "drive out the fear," Japanese workers and supervisors communicate openly and freely in scheduled meetings to discuss and promote the company's priority goals.

The success story of the top Japanese car manufacturers as explained by Dr. Deming's quality-control principle includes the critical productive two-way evaluation process. The concept of two-way evaluation distinguishes the world of K–12 education from the world of higher education. In K–12 education it is a common acceptable practice for only the teacher to evaluate the students in a formal manner. In higher or 13+ education the reciprocal evaluation between the professors and the students is the norm.

Figure 9.1 is a schematic representation of the two-way evaluation process in college teaching. The process has two major dimensions. The first one: the professor evaluates the students in terms of knowledge, skills, and attitude. The second one: the students reciprocally evaluate the professor also in terms of knowledge, skills, and attitude. Welcome to the world of accountability in higher education.

ASSESSMENT VERSUS EVALUATION

At the end of the school term, Dr. Berger pulls up the class assessment electronic spreadsheet on the computer screen. The spreadsheet has the class roster against seven assessment items aligned to the course syllabus. The items are attendance, class participation, assignments, projects, quizzes and tests, the midterm, and the final examination. After all the assessment information is entered, the total accumulative points are calculated swiftly by the application of a Microsoft Excel formula and the final student grades are determined.

Educators are not foreign to the accountability process of giving student grades. Do educators ask why the process takes so much time? Or, why does it take the entire school term to determine the final student grades? The

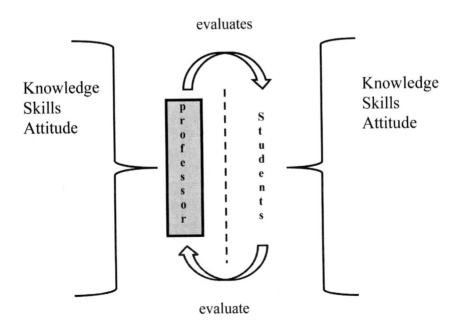

Figure 9.1. Full Circle Assessment Schema

answer is that it is a step-by-step approach to solving a challenging problem about learning. The step-by-step approach is the assessment and the problem is the determination of how much students have learned.

Similar to doing a science laboratory experiment, the experimenter meticulously collects information about the subject of investigation. Everything that has transpired and has been collected over time is included and considered. The process is called "assessment" and it is obviously the first step in an investigative process. The assessment data eventually accumulate to form the basis of the final evaluation. Switching from the laboratory back to the classroom, the teacher is the experimenter; the subjects of investigation are the students; the data are the assessment items described; finally, the problem is to identify the level of learning against a pre-determined criteria of A, B, C, D, and F, commonly known as the course grades.

The final course grade or evaluation points out whether the learners have met the objectives of the course. The final grade is the last part of the inquiry; it involves telling the students and the professors whether the goal of learning has been achieved or not. By comparing the outcomes with the formative data in the assessment, the professors form the basis of their final evaluation.

In summary, educational assessment and evaluation are the two interlocking phases of an inquiry process. Assessment is done at the formative stage of problem solving, whereas evaluation is usually done at the end. Assessment represents both objective and subjective data, while evaluation notes whether there have been changes or improvement in the overall data trend. In essence, there can be no evaluation without assessment and vice versa. Figure 9.2 illustrates the components of assessment and evaluation, and their relationships over time. *Assessment* is not to be confused and used interchangeably with *evaluation*. The nature of assessment is formative and it does not include making a final judgment, which is what evaluation does.

THE PROFESSOR EVALUATES STUDENTS

Professors are familiar with evaluating students using tests and quizzes. Many think of evaluation as a test of academic knowledge and skills. How often do professors think of student attendance assessment as something that is important, if not more important than assessing the academic subject? The professor needs to decide whether student attendance is a part of the final grade and this is not done without challenge. How can attendance be taken in a lecture hall with over a hundred students? That's just one example of the challenge. Maybe it is more practical to do that with a smaller class. Regardless of the attendance policy decision, put it down clearly in the syllabus (see chapter 2) and reinforce the policy on the first day of class (see chapter 4).

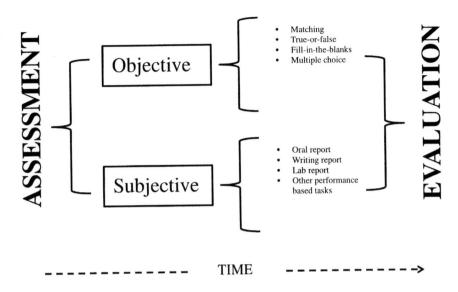

Figure 9.2. Assessment-Evaluation Continuum

Student attendance is the foundation for student learning for the simple reason that students need to come to class to learn. Poor attendance alerts the professor that the student is disengaging from learning. It may further reflect a lack of student motivation or lack of instructional support. There are attendance factors that the professor has little or no control over. On the other hand, there are other factors that the professor or the institution can change and help. Why should the professor care, and aren't the students adult enough to know what is good for them? Whether the professor cares or not depends on his/her work philosophy (see chapter 2). One easy way the professor can help is to refer the students to the student learning/success center if poor attendance is related to academic challenge.

A strategy that the professor can use to encourage attendance is to give students a taste of success. Students tend to repeat the same behavior of coming to class to achieve the same successful experience. Professors need to critically reflect and assess their own behavior to see if what they do is helping students. The professor can self-reflect on the following questions and find answers in chapters 3, 5, 6, 7, and 8.

1. Is the teaching engaging?
2. Is the class environment conducive to learning?
3. Is the professor being fair and consistent to students?
4. Does the professor address learning problems adequately?
5. Does the professor build on student success to boost confidence?

Assessment is commonly seen as either objective or subjective. Objective assessment is asking a question anticipating a single correct answer. In objective assessment the student chooses an answer from a list of possibilities. On the other hand, subjective assessment is asking a question anticipating more than one correct answer. In subjective assessment the students are asked to construct responses using verbal, acting, or written communication skills. There are various types of objective and subjective questions. Objective question types include true/false answers, multiple choice, multiple response, and matching questions. Subjective questions include extended-response questions, essays, and projects. How do professors decide on the appropriate use of objective and subjective tests? Let us explore further.

OBJECTIVE MEASUREMENT

Professors use a variety of methods to assess objectively. Objective assessments can be viewed as simple and frequent checks to monitor student learning. Informal assessments can be observing, listening, and asking probing questions beyond giving tests or quizzes. For example, after seeing a few students making the same computation mistakes in solving a problem, the professor might decide to offer help to the students making the mistakes so the rest of the class may restrategize their approach to solving the problem.

Professors are familiar with chapter or unit tests. Such assessments are meant to be formative and may constitute a certain predetermined percentage of the final grade as prescribed by the syllabus. Halfway through the school term, the professor commonly administers a midterm examination. At the end, the professor gives a comprehensive final examination.

The above assessments described are most frequently administered in the paper-and-pencil format. The format of the assessment may include fill-in-the-blanks, matching, true-or-false, and the ever-popular multiple-choice examination. The use of the multiple-choice examination is popular because it is easy to administer and score (by a machine), and it is objective because the answer is unambiguous. An objective test does not determine the quality of the answer but simply finds out whether the answer is correct or not correct.

Fill-in-the-Blank Questions

Fill-in-the-blank or completion questions are relatively easy to construct. They are quick checks covering many key conceptual terms. The downside of using fill-in-the-blank questions is the challenge of avoiding ambiguity (i.e., unanticipated but correct answers) and the low-level recall assessment of content or procedural knowledge (see chapter 5). Some practical suggestions for using this type of question are: (a) limit the number of blanks to one per question, (b) limit the response to single words or brief phrases, (c) give students credit for unanticipated yet correct responses, (d) let students know if spelling and grammar count, and (e) avoid giving grammatical clues such as the use of *a* or *an* before a blank. Use *a/an* instead.

Matching Questions

Matching questions test the recognition of simple understandings. The questions are constructed by two columns: a stem column and a response column. Some practical suggestions for using this type of question are: (a) put the stem column on the left and the response column on the right, (b) write the specific relationship between the stems and responses in the directions of the question (rework the question if the stem and the response do not flow), (c) order the responses in some logical way such as sequential or alphabetical, (d) keep the grammar consistent across stems and responses, and (e) provide more responses than stems.

True-or-False Questions

True-or-false questions are okay only for quick checks of vocabulary and concepts. Due to the 50/50 chance of scoring the correct answer, the point value assigned should be minimal. Some practical suggestions for using this type of question are: (a) use a single concept to determine the correct answer, (b) do not use negatives or, worse yet, double negatives, (c) avoid using qualifiers such as *generally*, *most*, *may*, *should*, and *often*, and (d) plan to have approximately 50 percent of the statements true and the remaining 50 percent false.

Multiple-Choice Questions

Multiple-choice questions are excellent to test a large number of concepts in a reasonable period of response time such as the midterm or the final examination. Questions can elicit responses from all cognitive levels (i.e., Bloom's Taxonomy in chapter 5) from recall to evaluation. A traditional multiple-choice question requires a student to choose one answer from a number of given choices.

A multiple-choice question has the following four basic components. The components are stem, choices, key (or correct answer), and distracters. Figure 9.3 illustrates the anatomy of a multiple-choice question. The stem is the text of the question. The choices are the options provided after the question stem. The key is the correct answer. The distracters are the incorrect answers embedded in the list of options.

Some practical suggestions for using this type of question are: (a) use the same number of distracters for every answer (in other words, keep it consistent to have the same number of choices for all the questions), (b) use only

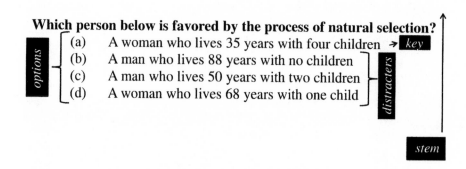

Figure 9.3.   Anatomy of a Multiple Choice Question

plausible distracters that are related to the question stem (ridiculous distracters are just "give away" options; common misconceptions are good distracters and distracters in figure 9.3 are examples), (c) write all the choices including the key approximately the same length (novice test writers tend to write keys that are longer than the distracters), (d) avoid wordiness and ambiguity, (e) change the position (i.e., A, B, C, D, etc.) of the answer key, (f) avoid using *none of the above* or *all of the above*, (g) do not use answer option like "A and C but not D and E" (multiple correct answers are seldom used, at least in high-stakes examinations), (h) use graphic support if it is too wordy to describe a question stem, and (i) develop knowledge and procedural questions that address various levels of cognition.

SUBJECTIVE MEASUREMENT

There are times when the use of objective testing is not applicable because the professor wants the students to compose/perform rather than selecting a response. Furthermore, the professor might want to assess the students' higher-order thinking skills (i.e., Bloom's Taxonomy in chapter 5), which would be an extreme challenge if an objective testing method is employed. For example, a philosophy professor may ask the student to explain with examples to illustrate how a person's failure is related to his ethical decisions. In a testing situation like such, using subjective methods like essay questions would be appropriate. In another example, a health professor may ask the student to demonstrate his competency in administering cardiopulmonary resuscitation—CPR. In a testing situation like this, using subjective methods like authentic performance tests would be appropriate.

Essay Questions

When should essay questions be used? The first step in considering whether to use essay questions is to determine the intended learning outcome that the test item is meant to assess. You may check the syllabus for course learning outcomes, assuming they are listed. Learning outcomes are stated in directive action verbs. Directive verbs such as *define, explain, analyze, synthesize, appraise,* and *create* are used to indicate what thought processes and actions students need to exhibit in order to demonstrate the evidence of learning.

"Create a solution to economic inequality in the United States" is an intended learning outcome in a Business 340 course syllabus. Here the directive verb *create* means "to put elements together to form a coherent and functional whole." Creating a solution to a problem requires higher-level critical thinking skills. Therefore, students' ability to create should be tested preferably with essay questions because they allow students' reasoning and coherence of thoughts to be analyzed by the professor. In essence, the directive verb in the learning outcome should be used to guide and focus the student responses to the performance to be assessed.

There are testing situations when it is a challenge to determine whether an objective method (i.e., multiple-choice questions) or a subjective method (i.e., essay questions) should be used. Compare the following two pairs:

1. What are the basic steps of cellular respiration?
2. Identify the basic steps of cellular respiration, and explain in your own words what happens in each step.
3. Should the World Exhibition ever be cancelled because of the potential threat of terrorism?
4. Decide whether the World Exhibition should ever be cancelled because of the threats of terrorism, and justify the decision.

In the above example, 1 and 2 are the first pair, 3 and 4 are the second pair. The first question in the pairs (i.e., 1 and 3) is best assessed by objective measures. The second question in the pairs (i.e., 2 and 4), on the other hand, is best measured by subjective measures such as essay questions. The subjective essay questions are preferred in questions 2 and 4 because the questions are meant to assess students' understanding of the subject-matter knowledge and their ability to reason with the knowledge.

Authentic Assessment

If you were to go to the airport, would you ask a friend who passed the written portion of the driver's license test to drive you? The answer is obvious, is it not? The person who passed the written test has the head knowledge of road signs and driving rules. Unfortunately, the written test shows no evidence that your friend can drive. To show that your friend is capable of driving, he also needs to take and pass the road test. The road test authentically assesses the person's skill from knowing to doing (i.e., driving).

Authentic assessment has other common names and they are performance assessment, alternative assessment, and direct assessment. These terms are used simply because students are asked to (1) *perform* meaningful tasks in real-world contexts, (2) take an *alternative* to traditional testing such as multiple-choice questions, and (3) provide more *direct* learning evidence of purposeful knowledge and skills. Authentic assessment can be used to test a skill such as driving. Nevertheless, can we say the same thing about testing academic subjects such as mathematics, science, and history? Professors can teach students how to do math, science, and history in addition to how to know about them. In this case, the professor can assess what students had learned and ask them to perform tasks that tackle the challenge faced by those applying mathematics, conducting science experiments, or analyzing historical events.

Let us study a Speech 207 class assignment to understand the construction of the authentic performance task and see how the quality of the performance is assessed by the use of a scoring rubric.

Authentic assessments are often about doing a task because they include real-world applications we ask students to perform. In a speech class assignment, students are asked to debate topics. The learning outcome of the speech assignment is to train students to articulate, justify, and prove their position on a topic. Let us examine two topics below.

1. Understanding what *charisma* means is important to future leaders of society. Future careers of the students will include the aspect of leadership. Is leadership possible without charisma?
2. U.S. society is preoccupied with the idea of success. Success means different things for different social groups and ages. To be successful at the age of sixteen is getting a driver's license. To be successful at the age of thirty-five means having your own house or business. How do luck, resources, and education play a role in reaching success?

The two topics are designed to be learning episodes for the student. The tasks are couched in real-world contexts of (1) leadership and charisma, and (2) paths to success. The two assignment topics are typical in that each starts with a context statement before asking the debate question. Obviously, there is no debate if the debaters take the same view or side of the topic. For that reason, the debaters need to take opposite views. A debate is a speech performance. For all practical purposes, a paper-and-pencil test would not be able to honestly assess the debate ability of a student. How then can a performance task such as debate be assessed? The answer is an assessment rubric (figure 9.4).

A rubric is a scoring tool that lists the judging criteria against the levels of performance. In figure 9.4 the five judging criteria on the left side of the matrix are information, understanding the topic, organization, use of facts or statistics, and presentation style. For each criterion, the evaluator using the

CATEGORY	4 points	3 points	2 points	1point
Information	All information presented in the debate was clear, accurate and thorough.	Most information presented in the debate was clear, accurate and thorough.	Most information presented in the debate was clear and accurate, but was not usually thorough.	Information had several inaccuracies OR was usually not clear.
Understanding of Topic	The team clearly understood the topic in-depth and presented their information forcefully and convincingly.	The team clearly understood the topic in-depth and presented their information with ease.	The team seemed to understand the main points of the topic and presented those with ease.	The team did not show an adequate understanding of the topic.
Organization	All arguments were clearly tied to an idea (premise) and organized in a tight, logical fashion.	Most arguments were clearly tied to an idea (premise) and organized in a tight, logical fashion.	All arguments were clearly tied to an idea (premise) but the organization was sometimes not clear or logical.	Arguments were not clearly tied to an idea (premise).
Use of Facts/Statistics	Every major point was well supported with several relevant facts, statistics and/or examples.	Every major point was adequately supported with relevant facts, statistics and/or examples.	Every major point was supported with facts, statistics and/or examples, but the relevance of some was questionable.	Every point was not supported.
Presentation Style	Team consistently used gestures, eye contact, tone of voice and a level of enthusiasm in a way that kept the attention of the audience.	Team usually used gestures, eye contact, tone of voice and a level of enthusiasm in a way that kept the attention of the audience.	Team sometimes used gestures, eye contact, tone of voice and a level of enthusiasm in a way that kept the attention of the audience.	One or more members of the team had a presentation style that did not keep the attention of the audience.

Figure 9.4. Authentic assessment rubric — debate

rubric can determine to what degree the student has met the criteria, that is, the level of performance on the top of the matrix. The rubric includes a mechanism for assigning a score to each criterion from four points to one point. A perfect performance would earn the student a total of twenty points, which, when multiplied by five, would conveniently convert the score to 100 percent.

Going back to the earlier example of asking a friend to drive to the airport brings home a very important guideline of assessment choices. The best choice of a qualified driver is to have a person who passed both the written and road tests knowing that he had a good knowledge base about driving (which might best be assessed by an objective multiple-choice test) and he applied the knowledge in a real-world context (demonstrating through a sub-jective authentic driving assessment). In the real world the written test uses the multiple-choice test format and the road test is a driving test. What, then, is the conclusion? The professor does not necessarily need to choose between objective and subjective assessment methods, of which there are many. They complement each other and are therefore not mutually exclusive.

TEST VALIDITY AND RELIABILITY

Objective or subjective test questions can be written either painstakingly or conveniently by copying the publisher's test bank (print or electronic). Re-gardless of the source, the test items need to align purposefully to the teach-ing, which in turn should align to the course syllabus (not the textbook) to achieve a very important property of testing—validity. Obviously, using the publisher's test bank purposelessly will not make the test valid.

Validity is considered to be a very important quality in testing. A valid test measures what it claims to measure, and a test that is not valid has no meaning. For example, a chapter 2 test is not a valid measurement for the content mastery of chapter 1; the chapter 2 test is therefore not valid and is useless. One simple rule to ensure the validity of any test is to follow the wisdom of "what you test is what you teach," period.

Veteran faculty may advise new faculty to develop at least two different but parallel forms of the same test, commonly known as form A and form B. What is the wisdom of the advice? Through time, test questions (and even assignments and projects) may pass from students to friends and siblings taking the same course. When "cheating" like this happens, the test will not serve the intended purpose of evaluation.

One big challenge facing the development of form A and form B of a test is the quality of being consistent. When the parallel forms of the same test are administered to the same group of test takers and the results are consistent, form A and form B are said to be consistent or reliable. This is analogous to weighing a 200-pound person on two scales. The two scales are extremely reliable when each records the weight as 200 pounds. If one scale reads 200 and the second scale reads 195; the second scale is not reliable.

The construction of two parallel test forms is very challenging. The task theoretically involves writing two different sets of questions aimed at testing similar concepts, and it is time consuming. Wait, there is a short cut. A professor may have a midterm examination with fifty test items. Can he not scramble the test items to make two forms? The scramble technique is commonly used when there are a large number of students sitting close to each other taking the same test. This way one row of students can take form A of the test and the next row of students can take form B of the same test.

On a similar note, if a test item has little or no power to discriminate (i.e., test item is either too difficult or too easy), it would be hard to distinguish between test takers who know the answer and those who do not. For example, if all (i.e., 100 percent) of the test takers answer a question correctly, that question has absolutely no discrimination power in measurement because the item is too easy. The reverse is also true when no one (i.e., 100 percent) can answer a test item correctly; that item is equally not useful because it is too difficult.

In test-item development, regardless of the type (i.e., objective or subjective) or form (i.e., fill-in-the-blank, matching, true-or-false, multiple-choice, essay questions, and authentic performance tests), the critical properties of being valid and reliable need to be meticulously held to make assessment and evaluation meaningful, accurate, and purposeful.

STUDENTS EVALUATE THE PROFESSOR

Toward the end of the school term and usually before the final examination the students will get to evaluate the professor. This evaluation is done anonymously using either paper and pencil or electronic format. The participation rate of the professor evaluation is usually less than 100 percent. Why? Are students not interested telling the professor what they think about the course and his teaching? The truth of the matter is that most students will take the time only if they have something good or especially bad to say.

What is the major purpose of faculty evaluation? The evaluation focuses on learning and the methods used to facilitate learning. In other words the evaluation measures the teaching effectiveness of the instructor. From the information, strengths and areas in need of improvement are suggested, while factoring out variables beyond the professor's control, such as class size, student motivation, and work habits. Now that the evaluation purpose is explained, it is more accurate to say that the students idealistically evaluate the professor's teaching and not so much the professor as a person.

Student ratings of teaching have been a major feature of the higher education landscape for more than three decades. Although there continue to be discussions over the use of and interpretation of the ratings, they are by far the common tool used in the evaluation of teaching. The rating of teaching consists essentially of two parts: the qualities of teaching and the methods of teaching.

Qualities of Teaching

To say that a student's rating of a professor is about his teaching is only a broad goal. Under the broad goal are specific objectives addressing the various teaching qualities. One classification of teaching qualities is:

1. Content knowledge:

    a. factual knowledge to include terminology, classifications, methods, and trends;
    b. learning principles to include theories, principles, and generalizations; and
    c. the application of knowledge to include decision making, problem solving, and critical thinking.

    The essence of the objective is the assessment of the professor's understanding of the central idea of teaching, methods of inquiry, and structures of the discipline and the provision of learning experiences that make the knowledge meaningful to the students.

2. Academic skills:

    a. communication skills, oral or written, to express oneself; and
    b. critical-thinking skills to analyze and evaluate concepts, arguments, and points of view.

    The essence of the objective is the assessment use of effective communication techniques and instructional techniques to foster active inquiry, collaboration, supportive interaction, problem solving, and learning in the classroom.

3. Specific skills:

    a. special skills related to the course and the subject matter;
    b. team collaboration skills; and
    c. creative skills.

The essence of the objective is the assessment use of the community of learners to support student learning and well-being in a way that is creative and relevant to the discipline.

4. Lifelong learning:

    a. using resources to solve problems and answer questions; and
    b. demonstrating the interest or passion of learning.

The essence of the objective is the assessment of the instructor as a reflective practitioner who actively seeks opportunities to grow professionally.

Methods of Teaching

Various individual methods of teaching are listed (see chapter 6) and some are used as a combination method (i.e., lecture and discussion, lecture and laboratory, etc.).

The institution might invite the faculty to predetermine the emphasis of the course with reference to objectives 1, 2, 3, and 4 in connection to the primary and secondary methods of teaching. Is it surprising to find that lecture and discussion are the popular primary and secondary methods of teaching? Lecture-laboratory is also a common combination method.

In the event that lecture and laboratory are the primary teaching approaches, professors are likely to emphasize the achievement of the content-knowledge objective. If discussion is the primary teaching approach, then professors are likely to emphasize general academic skills. While it is hard to tell whether qualities of teaching objectives dictate the methods of teaching, it is clear that the two are related.

THE UNIVERSITY EVALUATES THE PROFESSOR

The chapter of accountability is not complete if the institution is left out in the evaluation of the professor. After all, the rank and tenure committee of the institution evaluates in order to grant tenure and promotion to the teaching faculty. In the case of adjunct faculty, continuous good teaching evaluation is needed to sustain the job. There is a myth among teaching faculty that adjuncts and tenure-track faculty are more likely to be lenient to students (i.e., in assignment and grading) in their attempt to get good student evaluations. Some even claim there is a correlation between student grades and the level of professor evaluation to imply that a class with more As will result in a higher evaluation of the professor. This is still a perception at best.

Please note that, contractually, adjunct faculty are not eligible for tenure. Keeping the professional end goal (i.e., tenure) in mind is always helpful, though the new faculty will not have to worry too much about the tenure application until they are in their fifth or sixth year of teaching.

Faculty members preparing for the tenure application may start to collect artifacts of teaching, scholarship, and service early. Teaching artifacts may include video, evaluation, letters (to include emails), and note cards from students. Scholarship artifacts may include publications and conference presentations and proceedings. Service artifacts may include offices held with the university and professional organizations. Finally, the narration and the artifact support may go into a portfolio for the review committee. Nowadays, a professional electronic portfolio is preferred due to its convenient access and the easy navigation in using hyperlinks.

From the college/university perspective, faculty evaluation with reference to teaching (i.e., student ratings of instruction), scholarship (i.e., professional publication, grant writing, attending and presenting at professional conferences), and service (i.e., serving in professional organizations and college committees) is important to define the vitality and excellence of the institution in which the professor is employed.

SUMMARY AND REFLECTION

The two domains of accountability in higher education are professor initiated and student initiated. The effective professor needs to select a combination of methods to assess the performance of students. These methods include both objective and subjective strategies of measurement. The objective measurement options are fill-in-the-blank, matching, true-or-false, and multiple-choice tests. The subjective measurement options are essay and authentic performance tests. Regardless of the testing methods, it is absolutely critical that the instruments used are valid and reliable. In higher education the students also evaluate professors with reference to teaching qualities and the teaching methods used. The reciprocal assessment of the professors and students constitutes the full circle of accountability in higher education. The accountability of the students and the professors determines the excellence of the institution.

Consider the following self-reflective questions:

1. Assuming that you are already teaching, how would you assess your use of technology in teaching?
2. Assuming that you are using some form of instructional technology, how would you improve your level of effectiveness?
3. Understanding that the use of technology to enhance instruction is not an option, how would you incorporate new technology in your teaching?

About the Author

Ovid K. Wong is currently an associate professor at Benedictine University in Lisle, Illinois. He holds a joint appointment with the School of Education and the College of Science. He received his B.Sc. and Dip.Ed. from the University of Alberta in Canada, his M.Ed. from the University of Washington, Seattle, and his Ph.D. in curriculum and instruction from the University of Illinois. His experience in public education spans more than twenty years, from the urban classroom in Chicago to the suburban office of the assistant school superintendent. In 1989, Dr. Wong received the National Science Foundation's Outstanding Science Teacher in Illinois award and the Science Teaching Achievement Recognition (STAR) award from the National Science Teachers Association. In the same year, he visited the former Soviet Union as the science delegation leader with the student ambassador program. He was the first recipient of the outstanding alumni award from the University of Alberta in 1992 and the first recipient of the distinguished alumni award from the College of Education at the University of Illinois in 1995. In the summer of 2012 and 2013, Dr. Wong was invited by the Department of Foreign Expert Affairs in China to train young faculty at Dalian Nationalities University. He is the author of twenty-eight books and has received the Midwest Book Author award from the Children's Reading Roundtable of Chicago. His recent books are dedicated to coaching teachers and students to effectively prepare for the state-mandated examinations in Illinois and New York.